FOR EVERY SEASON

there is a dessert

FOR EVERY SEASON

there is a dessert

LINDA STEIDEL

Photography by Mark Choate

Brio Press
12 South Sixth Street #1250
Minneapolis, Minnesota 55402
www.briobooks.com

Manufactured in the United States of America

10 9 8 7 6 5 4 3 2 1

Edited by Cindy Choate
Book Design by Brio | Anthony Sclavi Minneapolis, MN
Photography by Mark Choate

ISBN 13: 978-1-937061-97-5
Library of Congress Control Number: 2011930769

acknowledgments

"Thank you" really seems inadequate for what it takes to put the books together. It's all about the team. We started the 'For Every Season' series with just a few guidelines. I wanted recipes that were easy to read and follow, but would always promise great results. Mark wanted photographs that were realistic and truly conveyed what the end result would be. Each recipe in the books has been prepared, photographed, then (the final test) eaten.

Cindy Choate is our editor and a biting critic (good choice of words). I am so grateful that she sees things that I never do. Linda Fasoli, my terrific business manager, allows me to focus on the creative side. She's the reason I sleep so well.

We are fortunate to have Brio Press as our publisher. From the very beginning we have all been on the same page. Anthony Sclavi, with his design and layout, continues to bring a touch of class and freshness.

'Salad' was first in the series followed by 'Pasta'. 'Dessert' was not the logical third book, but the unanimous choice of my students, and we listened to them.

Thank you all for your continued interest. We are having so much fun and looking forward to 'Hors d'oeuvres', the next in our series. I think you will love it.

I'd like to add a special thank you to Jennifer Payne. As the creative and technical force behind my beautiful website and Facebook page, she has truly been there for us.

Linda

The most fun for me, by far, is teaching a live class. Creating these cookbooks, though, could be a close second. Often, in class, I would ask students which book they would like to see next in the *For Every Season* series. Surprisingly to me, the most requested, hands down, was dessert. So, here it is, by popular demand, *For Every Season There is a Dessert!*

Desserts, I find in general, take a little more attention to detail and a little more quiet finesse than the other courses. For two reasons, though, they're worth the trouble. First, the dessert is a little surprise, a gift from the chef. Second, and more important, the dessert will be the last impression. We don't want to screw it up. It's the one last shot at adding a crescendo to a superb repast, or maybe turning around a presentation that turned out limp and needed a rescue. Whatever the preceding moments, desserts should be the secret weapons in the arsenal of any chef, whether amateur or professional. The sweet finale is one nice way to set yourself apart and assure a unique, memorable dining experience for your guests. In this collection, I paid my usual homage to seasonal foods, moods, and weather. Also, I thought it important to span the range of personal taste preferences. So, you should be able to explore the book, and find a few dessert designs that really hit you. Sometimes, by paying attention, maybe asking a few discreet questions, you can plan a special surprise for your guests with their very favorite dessert. So, with this book, more than any other in the series, I want to tell you to

. . . Have fun!

–Linda

the dessert is a little surprise, a gift from the chef

owner's manual

- Read each recipe through before beginning.
- Measure liquids in glass or clear plastic liquid-measuring cups.
- Measure dry ingredients in metal or plastic dry measuring cups that can be leveled off with a knife.
- Do not sift flour unless specified in a recipe. When sifted flour is called for, sift the flour before measuring it. Flour can vary by 50% or more according to how it is measured.
- "Large" eggs are labeled as such. Do not substitute.
- To measure solid fats (butter) pack them into a metal measuring cup or spoon pressing down to prevent air spaces, and then level them off.

chocolate a brief history

"So noble a confection, more than nectar and ambrosia, the true food of the gods." We tend to think of chocolate as a sweet, created recently. Actually, chocolate dates back to the ancient people of Mesoamerica. They drank chocolate as a bitter beverage. Chocolate was not a favorite food. The story of chocolate spans more than 2,000 years and now circles the globe. Chocolate took a role in religion and romance. Cultures around the world used chocolate and its botanical source to worship gods, win political favor, and woo loved ones. The Mayans and Aztecs took the harvested seeds and ground them into a paste. When mixed with water, chili peppers, cornmeal, and other ingredients, this paste made a frothy, spicy chocolate drink. As Europe started to import chocolate, they added cinnamon and sugar. Chocolate then became a symbol of wealth and power. The tale began in the tropical rainforests of Central and South America where cacao first grew. Chocolate is made from the seeds of the cacao tree. The truth be known, we love chocolate. The secret is and will always be the quality of the chocolate. Most chocolate desserts have very few ingredients, so the quality becomes the key. Choosing a favorite chocolate is a little like choosing a favorite wine. Be selective and you will find a new excitement in eating and cooking with chocolate.

vanilla

Vanilla is an incredible flavor that we may take for granted. It's fun to step back and take a look at nature's wonderful gift: vanilla. The vanilla plant, an orchid, originally came from Mexico. The vine is grown on a pole or some other support. The flower must be pollinated to produce the fruit. The method for doing this today was discovered by a 12-year-old plantation slave in 1841. It's interesting that vanilla is produced in exotic places like Madagascar and Indonesia, but it all started in Mexico. Even the prized Tahitian vanilla comes from plants that originated in Mexico. Vanilla flavor is vital to the success of most desserts. That's the good news. The bad news is that pure, real vanilla is expensive. The artificial stuff just doesn't compare to the real thing. There are over 250 unique ingredients in natural vanilla. The knockoffs are just a poor substitute. So don't scrimp on this one! 97% of vanilla flavoring worldwide is synthetic. Using the real thing, then, puts your dessert in the top 3% in terms of quality.

Vanilla: another love food? While not scientifically proven, vanilla is said to be an aphrodisiac because it raises the levels of adrenaline and epinephrine. Soft lights and low background music might be good with dessert.

sugar

In a collection of recipes such as these, sugar is the star attraction in every one. It is the one ingredient on every page of this book that has rewarded the palate since Alexander the Great discovered it in 327 B.C. That's almost 2,500 years ago. For centuries sugar has been used successfully to heal wounds. It actually dries the wound, preventing the growth of bacteria. Some fresh brownies in that first aid kit could come in very handy! Sugar is one of the only ingredients that is 100% fat free. It is the only taste that we desire from birth and it is an important source of carbohydrates, the body's natural supply of energy. So, this true health food should be consumed without guilt! The body converts sugar to blood glucose—the primary fuel for the brain? That's right: blood glucose. So that dessert you're contemplating might be the smart choice. Bananas Foster could be a very tasty way to raise your IQ. Who knew? Sugar: the food of romance? In 1492, Columbus sailed to the Canary Islands to pick up water and supplies for his voyage to the New World. While there, he fell in love with Beatriz, the Governor of the Islands and decided to stay for a while. As a farewell and thank you gift, she gave him some stalks of sugar cane. Columbus took his love gift on the historic voyage and introduced sugar to the Americas. I'm thinking the true food of love might be sugar.

soufflé secrets

1. A parchment or foil collar allows for a higher, more stable soufflé. Tie the string in a bow so you can remove it easily. Pour batter to very top of dish if using a collar; if not, fill to within an inch of top for large dishes. If not using a collar, make a groove in batter by running your thumb around edge of dish—the soufflé will rise in a top-hat shape.
2. Refrigerate or freeze buttered dishes—this will help soufflé to rise straight up.
3. Make sure all equipment that comes in contact with the egg whites (including your hands) is perfectly clean and dry—any grease or water will prevent whites from reaching full volume. Use lemon juice or vinegar to clean bowls and beaters, then rinse with cold water and dry.
4. A copper bowl produces the most stable beaten egg whites. It is almost impossible to overbeat them. Second choice is stainless steel, third is glass—never use plastic. Omit cream of tartar if using a copper bowl.
5. It's better to under-beat egg whites than to over-beat, so if you're unsure, quit while you're ahead.
6. If you want to do most of the work in advance, prepare base, press plastic wrap tightly against the surface, and refrigerate for up to two days. Rewarm in a double boiler. All that's left to do is beat the egg whites, fold them in, and bake.
7. Make sure the oven is fully heated before baking—preheat at least fifteen minutes. An oven thermometer is helpful, as the precise temperature is important when baking soufflés. Place oven rack in lower third of oven and remove others.
8. When done, the soufflé will be very puffy and golden brown. You'll get a creamy center if the soufflé quakes a little when you move the dish; bake a few more minutes if you like a drier soufflé.
9. A soufflé should be served straight from the oven, but you can keep it at its peak for up to five minutes by turning off oven and leaving the door ajar. Avoid drafts.

summer

almond, apricot & cream cheese crostata

1. To make the pastry, place the flour and salt into the bowl of a food processor. Pulse until combined. Add the butter and cream cheese until combined and pulls away from the sides of the work bowl. Roll out the pastry into a 14-inch round. Place on a parchment-lined cookie sheet.

2. Preheat the oven to 400 degrees. Blend almond paste and 3 tablespoons sugar in processor until finely chopped. Add cream cheese, egg yolk, and vanilla, and blend until filling is smooth. Spread filling over crust, leaving 1 ½-inch plain border. Arrange apricot quarters, rounded side down, in spoke pattern in 2 concentric circles on top of filling. Fold dough border up over edge of filling. Brush exposed apricots with warm jam. Sprinkle with remaining 1 ½ teaspoons sugar.

3. Bake crostata until crust is golden brown and apricots are tender and slightly browned, about 40 minutes. Sprinkle with crushed amaretti. Cool 30 minutes. Serve warm or at room temperature.

CREAM CHEESE PASTRY
- 1 ½ cups all-purpose flour
- ¼ teaspoon salt
- 4-ounce bar cream cheese
- 8 tablespoons butter

- ½ 7-ounce log almond paste
- 3 ½ tablespoons sugar, divided
- 3 ounces cream cheese, cut into ½-inch cubes
- 1 large egg yolk
- 1 teaspoon vanilla extract
- 5 to 6 large apricots, quartered, pitted
- ¼ cup apricot jam, heated
- 3 crushed amaretti cookies

serves 8

1. Cook blackberries, apple, flour, cinnamon and 6 tablespoons sugar in a 2-quart heavy saucepan over moderate heat, stirring frequently until mixture just boils and is thickened, about 5 minutes. Transfer to a shallow bowl to cool.

2. Preheat the oven to 375 degrees. Line two baking sheets with parchment.

3. Roll out half of dough to a ⅛-inch thickness on a lightly floured surface. Roll into 16x11-inch rectangle, and then trim to a 15x10-inch rectangle, reserving the scraps. Cut into 6 (5-inch) squares. Place a heaping tablespoon of the fruit filling in the center of each square. Moisten edges of the squares with milk and fold into triangles, pressing edges to seal. Transfer to a lined baking sheet, arranging them 1 inch apart. Press tines of a fork around edges of the triangle. Cut 6 more triangles in the same manner with remaining half of the dough and filling to make a total of 12 pies. There may be enough reserved scraps of dough to make an additional pie.

4. Brush triangles with milk and sprinkle with remaining 2 tablespoons sugar. Bake until pies are golden, about 30 minutes. Cool and serve with ice cream.

DOUBLE-CRUST PASTRY
Blend together flour, butter, shortening, and salt in the bowl of a food processor just until mixture resembles coarse meal. Drizzle in the ice water until it forms into dough. Do not overwork dough. Turn out the dough onto a work surface and follow instructions for the blackberry hand pies.

· 2 cups blackberries
· 1 large Golden Delicious apple, peeled and coarsely grated
· 2 tablespoons plus 1 teaspoon flour
· ¼ teaspoon cinnamon
· 8 tablespoons sugar
· 2 tablespoons milk

· Vanilla ice cream

DOUBLE-CRUST PASTRY
· 2 ½ cups all-purpose flour
· 1 ½ sticks cold unsalted butter, cut into ½-inch cubes
· ¼ cup cold vegetable shortening
· ½ teaspoon salt
· 5 to 7 tablespoons ice water

makes 12 small pies

cherry-almond tart

1. Preheat the oven to 350 degrees. Butter the bottom and sides of the tart pan. Set aside.

FOR THE PASTRY

1. In a medium-size bowl, combine the butter, sugar, salt, almond and vanilla extracts, and almonds. Stir with a spoon to blend. Gradually incorporate enough flour to form smooth, soft dough. The dough should resemble soft cookie dough. Place the dough in the center of the buttered pan. With the tips of your fingers, press the pastry evenly on the bottom and sides of the pan. The dough will be quite thin. Place the tart pan on a parchment paper-lined sheet pan and place in the center of the oven. Bake until the dough is just slightly puffy and turns a very pale brown, about 10 minutes. Remove from the oven and set aside. Do not turn off the oven.

FOR THE FILLING

1. In a small bowl, combine the cream, egg, and almond and vanilla extracts; whisk to blend. Stir in the sugar, flour, ground almonds, and Kirsch.

2. Sprinkle 2 tablespoons of ground almonds on top of the prebaked pastry shell. (They will prevent the crust from becoming soggy.)

3. Arrange the cherries in a single layer in the pastry shell. Pour the filling over the cherries. Sprinkle with the remaining 2 tablespoons of ground almonds. Place in the center of the oven and bake until the filling is firm and the pastry is a deep golden brown, about 45 minutes. Remove and place on a rack to cool. Sprinkle with confectioners' sugar just before serving.

PASTRY
· 8 tablespoons butter, melted, plus additional for preparing tart pan
· ½ cup sugar
· Pinch of salt
· ⅛ teaspoon almond extract
· ⅛ teaspoon vanilla extract
· 2 tablespoons finely ground almonds
· 1 ¼ cups plus 1 tablespoon all-purpose flour

FILLING
· 5 tablespoons heavy cream
· 1 large egg, lightly beaten
· ½ teaspoon almond extract
· ½ teaspoon vanilla extract
· ¼ cup sugar
· 1 tablespoon all-purpose flour
· 2 tablespoons finely ground almonds
· 1 tablespoon Kirsch
· 4 tablespoons finely ground almonds
· 1 pound fresh cherries, pitted
· Confectioners' sugar, for garnish

serves 8

chilled grand marnier soufflé with marinated summer fruit

1. Put the cold water and the Grand Marnier into a small, heat-proof glass bowl. Sprinkle the gelatin over the liquid. Place the bowl in a small saucepan and add about an inch of water to the pan. Bring the water in the pan to a boil and let the heat of the boiling water dissolve the contents of the bowl. When the gelatin mixture seems quite dissolved, remove it from the pan and set it aside to cool.

2. Put the eggs and yolks into a bowl for the electric mixer. Set the whites aside in a clean, dry bowl. Begin beating the eggs and yolks together and gradually add the sugar, continuing to beat at high speed until the mixture is thick and very pale. Beat in the gelatin mixture and the vanilla. Set this mixture aside.

3. Whip the heavy cream in a chilled bowl until it is thick and stiff. Fold it gently into the egg mixture.

4. Whip the egg whites with the salt until they hold firm, stiff peaks. Fold them gently into the egg mixture. Tear off a long strip of aluminum foil or wax paper and fold it in half lengthwise. Butter one side and tie it around a 4-cup soufflé dish, buttered side in. Spoon the soufflé mixture into the prepared dish, allowing it to come up beyond the rim into the collar. Chill for at least 6 hours, or overnight.

5. Wash, hull, and slice the berries. Peel and cut the oranges into segments. Drizzle the Grand Marnier over the mixture and allow it to marinate for several hours.

6. To serve, carefully run a clean knife between the collar and the soufflé in the dish and pull the collar gently away. Garnish with the grated lime zest and serve the soufflé with the marinated fruit on the side.

· ¼ cup cold water
· ¼ cup Grand Marnier plus extra for drizzling over the berries
· 2 tablespoons unflavored gelatin
· 4 large eggs plus 3 additional eggs, separated
· ¾ cup sugar
· 1 teaspoon vanilla extract
· 2 cups heavy cream
· A dash of salt
· 1 pint fresh strawberries
· 3 - 4 large navel oranges
· Grated lime zest for garnish

serves 8

chocolate chip oatmeal cookies with rocky road ice cream

- · 2 sticks unsalted butter, softened
- · 1 cup packed light brown sugar
- · 1 cup granulated sugar
- · 3 large eggs
- · 2 teaspoons vanilla extract
- · 3 cups old-fashioned rolled oats
- · 2 cups all-purpose flour
- · 1 teaspoon baking soda
- · 1 teaspoon ground cinnamon

makes about 3 dozen 3-inch cookies

Your favorite cookie + your favorite ice cream = a perfect ice cream sandwich. Make them ahead of time and freeze them for an easy summer dessert.

1. Preheat the oven to 350 degrees. Line two baking sheets with parchment paper.

2. Cream the butter, brown sugar, and granulated sugar together in a large bowl with an electric mixer on high speed until fluffy. Add the eggs, one at a time, scraping down the sides of the bowl and blending thoroughly after each addition. Stir in the vanilla.

3. In a separate large bowl, combine the oats, flour, baking soda, cinnamon, and salt; stir to mix. Add to the creamed butter-sugar mixture and stir just until the dry ingredients are moist and blended in. Stir in the chocolate chips.

4. Scoop the dough out with a ¼ cup measure or ice cream scoop and drop it onto the prepared baking sheet, leaving about 3 inches between the cookies. Press the cookies to ½ inch thickness with the palm of your hand or the back of a spatula.

5. Bake the cookies on a center rack for 12 to 14 minutes for soft, chewy cookies, or 15 to 17 minutes for crunchy cookies, rotating the pans halfway through so the cookies bake evenly. Allow the cookies to cool on the baking sheet for about 5 minutes before transferring them to a cooling rack to cool completely. Place 6 cookies on a baking sheet that will fit in the freezer.

6. Scoop the ice cream with a ¼ cup measure or ice cream scoop and place one heaping scoop of ice cream on each of the cookies. Top each with another cookie, so the top of the cookie is facing up, and gently press down on the top cookie until the ice cream spreads out to the edge of the sandwich. Place the sandwiches on the baking sheet and repeat with the remaining sandwiches.

7. Cover the baking sheet tightly with plastic and freeze until the ice cream is firm, about 2 hours, or wrap the sandwiches individually and keep them frozen for up to 1 month.

1. Place the flour, salt, and sugar in the bowl of a food processor. Pulse until combined. Cut the cream cheese and butter into pieces and add one at a time, pulsing until dough forms into a ball. Divide the dough into 2 pieces. Refrigerate for about 30 minutes.

2. Remove from the refrigerator and roll out one piece on a lightly floured work surface into a 10-inch round. Lay it into a deep 9-inch pie pan or a 10-inch tart pan. Trim the edges. Cover and freeze for 10 minutes. Put the filling into the pastry shell and roll out the second piece of dough. Lay the dough over the filling and crimp the pastry edges together. You may want to cut the dough into strips to make a lattice top as an alternative.

3. Preheat the oven to 350 degrees. Bake for 25 to 30 minutes.

4. Whip the cream in a bowl with remaining sugar until soft peaks form and serve the pie with a dollop of whipped cream on top.

PEACH FILLING
Mix the peaches with ½ cup of the sugar, flour, cinnamon and pinch of salt. Spoon into the pastry- lined pie or tart pan.

CREAM CHEESE DOUBLE CRUST
· 2 ½ cups all-purpose flour
· ½ teaspoon salt
· ½ cup sugar
· 8 ounces cream cheese
· 10 tablespoons unsalted butter

PEACH FILLING
· 5 cups peeled, pitted, sliced peaches
  (about 2 to 3 pounds or 6 to 8 peaches)
· ¾ cups sugar, divided
· 3 teaspoons flour
· ¼ teaspoon cinnamon
· Pinch of salt
· 1 cup heavy cream

serves 8

cornmeal cake with peaches in red wine sangria

1. Preheat the oven to 350 degrees. Line the bottom of an 8-inch round cake pan with parchment paper and lightly oil.

2. Sift the cornmeal, flour, baking powder, and salt together in a bowl and set aside.

3. With an electric mixer, beat the sugar, eggs, and egg whites in a large bowl until smooth. Beat in the butter, oil, yogurt, lemon zest, and lemon juice until creamy. Fold in the dry ingredients just until combined; do not over mix.

4. Pour the batter into the prepared pan and smooth the top with a spatula. Bake for 35-40 minutes or until a toothpick inserted in the center comes out clean. Cool for 15 minutes on a wire rack. Invert, peel off the paper, and cool completely. (The cake can be made in advance and stored, wrapped in plastic wrap in the refrigerator for up to 5 days or frozen for 1 month.) Serve with peaches in red wine sangria.

PEACHES IN RED WINE SANGRIA
In a medium nonreactive saucepan, combine the wine, orange juice, sugar, brandy, cinnamon stick, and orange and lemon zests. Bring to a boil over high heat, then reduce the heat and simmer for 5 minutes. Pour the sangria into a heat-proof bowl and add the peaches. Let cool, then refrigerate for 5-6 hours before serving.

CAKE
- 1 cup yellow cornmeal
- ½ cup all-purpose flour
- 1 ½ teaspoons baking powder
- ¼ teaspoon salt
- 1 cup sugar
- 2 large eggs, 2 large egg whites
- 2 tablespoons unsalted butter, softened
- ¼ cup vegetable oil
- ½ cup plain yogurt
- 1 ½ tablespoons grated lemon zest
- 2 tablespoons fresh lemon juice

PEACHES IN RED WINE SANGRIA
- 2 cups dry red wine
- 1 cup fresh orange juice
- 1 cup sugar
- 2 tablespoons brandy
- 1 small cinnamon stick
- 2 long strips orange zest
- 5 peaches , cut into wedges

serves 8

This Spanish dessert is best when peaches are at their peak.

adriatic lemon sea breeze

In a blender, mix the ice cream, lemon juice, and vodka until it is smooth and pourable, about 1 minute. Pour into the martini glasses and garnish with a twist of lemon.

· 1 pint vanilla ice cream, softened at room temperature for 20 minutes
· 7 tablespoons fresh lemon juice
· ½ cup vodka
· 6 slices lemon peel
· Martini glasses for serving

serves 6

blueberry and peach cobbler with vanilla ice cream

- 2 cups blueberries
- 2 pounds fresh peaches, peeled and sliced
- ½ teaspoon grated lemon zest
- 5 tablespoons sugar, divided
- 2 cups plus 1 tablespoon cake flour
- 1 tablespoon baking powder
- Pinch of salt
- 5 tablespoons butter, cut into bits
- ¾ cup plus 1 tablespoon heavy cream

1. Preheat the oven to 400 degrees.

2. Combine the blueberries and sliced peaches in a bowl. Toss with the lemon zest, 4 tablespoons sugar, and 1 tablespoon flour. Transfer the fruit to a deep, 10-inch oven-proof serving dish.

3. To make the pastry, sift together the 2 cups cake flour, baking powder, and salt in a large bowl. Combine the butter with the flour until the mixture resembles coarse meal. Using a light touch, stir in ¾ cup cream to make soft and tender dough.

4. Turn the dough out onto a table and roll ¾ inch thick. With a cookie cutter, cut out 3-inch rounds. Arrange the rounds on top of the blueberries and peaches and brush with 1 tablespoon heavy cream. Sprinkle remaining 1 tablespoon sugar on top.

5. Bake for 30 to 35 minutes, until bubbly and lightly browned.

6. Serve warm with whipped cream or a scoop of vanilla ice cream.

chocolate waffles with raspberry coulis & ice cream

1. In the top of a double boiler, melt the butter and chocolate. In a separate bowl, whip the egg yolks and the brown sugar together. Cool the chocolate mixture slightly, for approximately 5 to 10 minutes, add it to the egg yolk mixture, and combine. Add the cognac and flour, mixing with a wire whisk. Refrigerate the batter until thickened, about 2 hours.

2. Place the raspberries and raspberry jam in the bowl of a food processor and puree. Add the Grand Marnier. Pass the mixture through a fine sieve to remove the seeds and set the sauce aside.

3. Preheat a well-greased waffle iron. In the bowl of an electric mixer, whip the egg whites until soft peaks form. Add the granulated sugar and whip slowly until the whites are firm but still moist. Whip the chocolate mixture until it is somewhat liquefied and stir in half of the egg whites. Fold in the remaining egg whites.

4. Cook the mixture in the waffle iron and serve the waffles immediately. Place a waffle on a plate, top with a spoonful of raspberry coulis and a dollop of ice cream and garnish with raspberries.

· 1 ¼ cups (2 ½ sticks) unsalted butter
· ¾ pound bittersweet chocolate
· 6 eggs, separated
· ½ cup brown sugar
· ¼ cup cognac
· 1 cup cake flour, sifted
· ½ cup granulated sugar

RASPBERRY COULIS
· 1 cup raspberries
· ½ cup seedless raspberry jam
· 1 tablespoon Grand Marnier

· Vanilla ice cream
· Raspberries for garnish

serves 6

These waffles freeze well. Make extra and have them for a quick dessert. The waffles are also great with coffee ice cream and hot fudge.

crème brûlée cheesecake with fresh berries

1. Preheat the oven to 350 degrees.

2. Prepare a water bath: place a 9x13-inch metal baking pan in the oven and fill with 1 inch of hot water. Place sugar in an 8-inch round metal cake pan with 2-inch tall sides and caramelize by placing on stovetop over medium heat. Watch for bubbles to form and allow sugar to melt and turn golden. Do not burn sugar. Remove from heat and set aside on wire rack.

3. Place cheesecake ingredients in a blender and blend at medium speed until smooth. Pour cheesecake mixture into sugar-glazed pan. It will fill pan to the rim.

4. Place cheesecake in water bath in oven. Bake for 1 hour or until top is set and golden. Carefully remove cheesecake from water bath and cool on wire rack.

5. When cool, cover and refrigerate for at least one hour, or overnight. To serve, run knife around edge of cake to loosen and invert onto serving platter. You may need to press on the bottom of the pan to loosen. Some caramelized sugar will remain in pan. Serve with fresh berries.

· 1 cup sugar
· 1 13-ounce can evaporated milk
· 16 ounces cream cheese
· 1 cup sugar
· 4 eggs
· 1 tablespoon vanilla
· Raspberries, blackberries, and blueberries

serves 8

This recipe combines crème brulee and cheesecake, two of my favorite desserts, and it is always a hit!

cast-iron peach cobbler with ice cream

1. Preheat the oven to 375 degrees.

2. Mix ½ cup flour, peaches, ⅓ cup sugar, 2 tablespoons butter, vanilla, ½ teaspoon salt, cinnamon, and nutmeg in a large bowl, tossing well. Spoon into a large cast-iron skillet. Add ½ cup water.

3. Combine remaining 1 cup flour, ⅓ cup sugar, ¼ teaspoon salt, and baking powder in a medium bowl; cut in ¼ cup butter with a pastry blender until mixture resembles coarse meal. Add buttermilk; stir just until moist. Drop batter by tablespoonfuls over peach mixture.

4. Bake at 375 degrees for 1 hour or until bubbly and browned. Serve warm with vanilla ice cream.

· 1 ½ cups flour, divided
· 6 large peaches, peeled and cut into slices
· ⅔ cup sugar, divided
· 2 tablespoons butter, melted
· 2 teaspoons vanilla
· ¾ teaspoon salt, divided
· ½ teaspoon ground cinnamon
· ¼ teaspoon nutmeg
· ½ cup water
· 2 teaspoons baking powder
· ¼ cup chilled butter, cut into small pieces
· 1 cup buttermilk
· Vanilla ice cream

serves 8

Make this dessert when peaches are at their peak. Serve right from the skillet with homemade ice cream.

raspberry tarts with meringue

1. Preheat the oven to 350 degrees. Line a 9x13-inch baking pan with foil, leaving 4 inches of overhang at the ends.

2. In a medium bowl, using an electric mixer beat the butter with ½ cup of the granulated sugar at high speed until fluffy, 3 to 5 minutes. Reduce the speed to low, add the flour and salt, and beat just until blended, 2 to 3 minutes. Press the dough into the baking pan in an even layer. Score the shortbread lengthwise into thirds, and then score crosswise 4 times to make 12 squares. Bake for 20 to 25 minutes, or until lightly browned. Transfer the pan to a rack and let the shortbread cool completely, about 1 hour. Lift the shortbread out of the pan. Spread the jam evenly over the shortbread. Using a serrated knife cut the shortbread into 12 squares following the score lines. Transfer the shortbread squares to a large baking sheet.

3. In a large stainless steel bowl set over a pan of simmering water, stir the egg whites with the remaining 1 ½ cups of granulated sugar until the sugar dissolves, about 1 minute. Remove the bowl from the heat. Using an electric mixer beat the whites at medium speed until frothy. Increase the speed to high and beat until a stiff, glossy meringue forms, about 5 minutes longer.

4. Spoon ½ cup of the meringue onto each of the squares. Using the back of a spoon, pull up the meringue to form high spikes. Bake for 20 to 25 minutes, or until the meringue is golden brown. Let cool for 10 minutes on the baking sheet on a rack, then transfer the tarts to the rack and let cool completely. Sift confectioner's sugar over the tops before serving.

· 2 sticks unsalted butter, softened
· 2 cups granulated sugar, divided
· 2 cups all-purpose flour
· ⅛ teaspoon salt
· ¾ cup seedless raspberry jam
· 8 large egg whites
· Confectioners' sugar, for dusting

makes 12 tarts

kirsch roulade with raspberry coulis & summer berries

FOR THE ROULADE

1. Preheat the oven to 350 degrees. Butter a 15x10-inch jelly roll pan. Press a sheet of parchment paper into the buttered pan. Butter the parchment paper well.

2. In a large bowl, using an electric mixer beat the egg yolks, sugar, and vanilla on high speed for about 2 minutes, until thick and pale. Incorporate the flour with a whisk.

3. In another bowl beat the egg whites on high speed until stiff peaks form. Whisk ¼ of the whites into the egg yolk mixture, then gently fold in the remaining whites with a large rubber spatula. Transfer the batter to the prepared pan and spread it evenly onto the corners. Bake in the middle of the oven for about 10 minutes, until evenly golden. Let the cake cool on a rack for 30 minutes.

4. Hold the parchment paper at each end and lift the cake out onto a work surface. Sprinkle the cake evenly with the Kirsch and spread the ½ cup preserves in a thin layer over the entire surface. Beginning at one of the short ends, grasp the parchment paper with both hands, and push and roll the cake into a neat, tight scroll, peeling off the paper as you go. When the cake is compactly rolled, rewrap it in the parchment and refrigerate for at least 1 hour to firm it up.

ROULADE

· 1 teaspoon butter
· 6 large eggs, separated
· ½ cup sugar
· 1 teaspoon vanilla extract
· ½ cup flour
· 1 ½ tablespoons kirsch
· ½ cup seedless raspberry preserves

COULIS

· 1 pound frozen raspberries
· 1 cup seedless raspberry preserves

· 12 large fresh strawberries, hulled and cut into 6 wedges
· ½ cup small fresh mint leaves
· 1 cup chilled creme fraiche

For maximum volume beat egg whites at room temperature in glass or metal bowl. This roulade can be filled with lemon curd or any jam of your choice.

FOR THE COULIS:

1. In a food processor, puree the raspberries with the 1 cup raspberry preserves. Press the puree through a fine sieve to remove seeds.

2. To assemble, spoon a few tablespoons of coulis onto dessert plates and tilt to coat evenly. Using a sharp knife, cut the roulade in 1-inch thick slices and place one in the center of each plate. Scatter the fresh berries around the cake. Arrange a few mint leaves between the berries and dot with dollops of crème fraiche. Serve immediately.

classic spanish flan with strawberries

1. Preheat the oven to 325 degrees.

2. Put 1 cup of the sugar into a heavy saucepan and add the water. Bring to a boil. Do not stir. Continue to cook until it begins to caramelize and turn amber, thick and bubbly. Immediately pour liquid caramel into a 10-inch pie dish or cake pan. Swirl it around to completely cover the bottom. Set aside to harden while you make the custard.

3. Zest the orange and put it into a saucepan with the cinnamon sticks and the half and half. Bring this just to the scalding point, remove from heat and let it stand, to blend the flavors. Be sure to strain out the zest and cinnamon before using.

4. Put the eggs, yolks, ½ cup sugar, and salt into a bowl and mix until smooth. Add the vanilla and slowly pour in the strained hot milk. Mix well.

5. Pour this mixture over the caramel and gently set the pan into a water bath or bain-marie.

6. Place in the oven and pour boiling water into the bain-marie until it comes halfway up the side of the pan. Bake the flan for 1 hour or until a clean knife inserted in the center of the custard comes out clean. Remove from the oven and carefully lift out of the bain-marie. Let the custard cool to room temperature. Chill overnight.

7. To serve the flan, run a knife around the edge of the custard to loosen. Carefully invert onto a serving platter that has shallow sides to contain the caramel, which will run as a liquid over the flan. Serve with the strawberries.

· 1 ½ cups sugar, divided
· ¼ cup water
· 1 large navel orange
· 2 cinnamon sticks
· 3 cups half and half
· 6 eggs plus 4 yolks
· Pinch of salt
· 1 teaspoon vanilla
· 1 pint fresh strawberries, washed and hulled

serves 8

grilled pineapple with blueberries, butter-rum glaze, & vanilla mascarpone

1. Combine the rum, butter, and sugar in a small saucepan and simmer, whisking often, until the sugar has melted and the mixture is slightly thickened, about 10 minutes.

2. Cut the vanilla bean lengthwise in half and scrape out the seeds with the tip of a sharp knife. Whisk the mascarpone and vanilla seeds together.

3. Heat the grill to high.

4. Grill the pineapple slices, brushing frequently with the glaze, 2 to 3 minutes per side, until browned.

5. Remove the pineapple to a platter or serving plates and top each slice with a few fresh blueberries. Add a spoonful of vanilla mascarpone. Drizzle with any remaining glaze. Serve immediately.

· 1 cup dark rum
· 12 tablespoons (1 ½ sticks) unsalted butter
· ¼ cup light brown sugar
· 1 vanilla bean
· 8 ounces mascarpone
· 1 ripe pineapple, peeled and sliced into ¼ -inch thick rounds
· ½ cup fresh blueberries

serves 6

autumn

apple spring rolls with caramel sauce & powdered sugar

1. Peel, core, and cut the apples into ½-inch chunks. In a 1-quart sauté pan add the sugar and let it begin to caramelize. Add the apples and sauté until golden. Add the butter, cinnamon, ginger, nutmeg, and scraped ½ vanilla bean. Then add the Calvados. Cook until the apples are tender. Remove from the heat and add 1 tablespoon sugar, lemon juice, and the pinch of salt.

2. Scoop out ½ of the sautéed apples with all of their liquid. Place in a food processor. Process until smooth. Remove from the food processor, combine with remaining apples and raisins.

3. Place the spring roll wrappers down on the table with the point facing you. Spoon 3 tablespoons of apple mixture in a line 2 inches from the bottom point. Fold up like a burrito.

4. Fry in 350 degree oil for 2 minutes, turning until golden on all sides. Remove and place on paper towels. Dust with confectioners' sugar and serve with caramel sauce.

CARAMEL SAUCE

Combine the sugar and ½ cup water in a 2-quart saucepan set over medium heat. Without stirring, cook mixture until dark amber in color, swirling the pan carefully while cooking, about 15 to 20 minutes. Reduce the heat to low. Slowly add the cream, stirring with a wooden spoon. Scrape the vanilla seeds into the pan and add the pod. Add the lemon juice and the butter. Stir to combine. Cover and store, refrigerated, up to 1 week. Remove the vanilla pod and bring sauce to room temperature or warm over low heat before serving.

· 6 small Granny Smith apples
· ⅓ cup sugar
· 6 tablespoons butter
· ⅛ teaspoon ground cinnamon
· ⅛ teaspoon ground ginger
· ⅛ teaspoon ground nutmeg
· ½ vanilla bean
· 2 tablespoons Calvados brandy
· 1 tablespoon sugar
· 1 teaspoon lemon juice
· Pinch salt
· ½ cup raisins
· Spring roll wrappers

CARAMEL SAUCE
· 2 cups sugar
· ½ cup water
· 1 cup heavy cream
· 1 vanilla bean, split in
  half lengthwise
· 2 teaspoons freshly
  squeezed lemon juice
· 2 tablespoons butter

serves 6

When caramelizing sugar, you cannot stir the sugar and water. If you do, it will instantly seize. Swirl the pan and wait for it to turn amber.

chocolate & almond zuccotto

1. Spray a 1 ½-quart bowl with nonstick cooking spray. Line the bowl with plastic wrap. Cut the pound cake crosswise into ⅓-inch-thick slices. Cut each slice diagonally in half, forming 2 triangles. Line the bottom and sides of the prepared bowl with the cake triangles. Brush some of the brandy over the cake triangles lining the bowl. Reserve extra triangles.

2. Stir the chocolate in a large metal bowl, set over a saucepan of simmering water until the chocolate melts. Remove from the heat and allow the chocolate to cool slightly. Using an electric mixer beat 1 cup of cream in another large bowl until stiff peaks form. Fold ¼ of the whipped cream into the chocolate. Fold half of the remaining whipped cream until combined. Fold in the remaining whipped cream. Spread the chocolate cream over the cake, covering the bottom and sides, creating a well in the center. Cover and refrigerate, if not assembling cake right away.

3. In a clean large bowl, add the remaining 1 cup of cream and almond extract. Beat on medium speed and gradually add the powdered sugar. Beat until firm. Fold in the toasted almonds. Spoon the cream mixture into the center of the well of the filling.

4. Brush the remaining cake slices with brandy. Arrange them brandy side down over the cake, covering completely and trimming to fit, if necessary. Cover the cake with plastic wrap and refrigerate for 4 hours or up to 1 day.

5. Invert the cake onto a platter. Remove the bowl and the plastic wrap. Sift the cocoa powder over, cut into wedges and slice.

- Nonstick cooking spray
- 1 (12-ounce) loaf pound cake
- ¼ cup brandy
- 6 ounces bittersweet chocolate, chopped
- 2 cups chilled whipping cream, divided
- ½ teaspoon pure almond extract
- ¼ cup powdered sugar
- ½ cup sliced almonds, toasted, coarsely crumbled
- Unsweetened cocoa powder

serves 8 - 10

CAKE
- 6 ounces bittersweet chocolate, coarsely chopped
- ⅔ cup (1 ½ sticks) unsalted butter
- ⅔ cup port
- 4 large eggs, separated
- 1 cup plus 4 tablespoons sugar
- 1 cup all-purpose flour
- Pinch of salt

GLAZE
- 1 cup heavy cream
- 8 ounces bittersweet chocolate, chopped

CHANTILLY CREAM
- 2 ¼ cups heavy cream
- 1 teaspoon vanilla extract
- 1 ½ tablespoons sugar
- Small pinch of salt

serves 8 to 10

If you have to chop a lot of chocolate, use a serrated knife. It's so much easier.

drunken chocolate cake with port & chantilly cream

1. Preheat the oven to 350 degrees. Line the bottom of a 9-inch round cake pan with parchment paper. In a double boiler over simmering water combine the chocolate, butter, and port. Heat, stirring occasionally, until smooth. Set aside and let cool to lukewarm. Combine the egg yolks and ½ cup plus 3 tablespoons of sugar in the bowl of an electric mixer. Beat on high speed until thick, about 3 minutes. Decrease the speed to medium-low and stir in the chocolate mixture. Stir in the flour and salt.

2. In a large bowl, beat the egg whites with the clean whisk attachment at medium speed until frothy. Increase the speed to high and beat until soft peaks form. Add the remaining ½ cup and 1 tablespoon sugar and continue beating until stiff, glossy peaks form. Stir one-third of the egg white mixture into the chocolate batter. Gently fold in the remaining whites. Pour the batter into the prepared pan. Bake until a toothpick inserted in the center comes out clean, 30 to 35 minutes. Remove from the oven, let cool and unmold.

3. To make the glaze, bring the cream to a boil in a heavy saucepan. Remove from heat and whisk in the chocolate until smooth. Let cool to room temperature and frost the sides and top of the cake. Let the cake stand for at least 1 hour before cutting.

4. One hour before serving, make the cream. In a large stainless-steel bowl, combine the cream, vanilla, sugar, and salt. Beat with a whisk just until it holds its shape. Refrigerate until ready to use. Whisk a few more times before serving.

5. To serve, cut the cake into slices with a knife dipped into hot water and dried. Dollop Chantilly cream on each piece.

bananas foster gratin with almond biscotti

1. Preheat the oven to 450 degrees. Lightly oil eight 1 to 1 ½-cup gratin dishes or a shallow 1-quart baking dish.

2. In a medium saucepan combine brown sugar, water, rum, and cinnamon; bring to a simmer, stirring. Remove from the heat and stir in the butter.

3. Peel the bananas and slice diagonally. Add to the sauce and toss to coat. Spoon into prepared dishes. Sprinkle with biscotti crumbs.

4. Bake gratins for about 10 minutes, or until bubbly. Serve hot or warm with a scoop of ice cream.

· ½ cup packed light brown sugar
· 6 tablespoons water
· 2 tablespoons dark rum or fresh lemon juice
· ½ teaspoon ground cinnamon
· 4 teaspoons butter
· 8 medium bananas
· 2 almond biscotti, crushed (½ cup)
· 1 pint vanilla bean ice cream

serves 8

CANDIED ZEST
· 4 thick-skinned oranges,
  such as navels
· ½ cup sugar

CHOCOLATE MOUSSE
· 4 ounces semisweet or bittersweet
  chocolate, chopped
· 2 ounces unsweetened chocolate,
  chopped
· ¼ cup Grand Marnier
· 3 tablespoons water
· 4 large eggs, separated
· 2 tablespoons sugar
· 1 cup heavy cream

ORANGE CREAM
· ¾ cup heavy cream
· 1 tablespoon Grand Marnier

serves 6
.

1. To make the candied zest: remove the zest from the oranges in long thin strips, using a 5-hole citrus zester. Bring a small saucepan of water to a boil, add the zest, and boil for 1 minute. Drain off the water and reserve the zest. Return the empty saucepan to the stove, add the sugar and ½ cup water, and bring to a boil over medium-high heat, stirring occasionally to dissolve the sugar.

2. Add the blanched zest to the syrup, reduce to a simmer, and cook until tender, about 5 minutes. Remove the saucepan from the heat and allow the zest to cool in the syrup, then strain, reserving both the candied zest and 1 tablespoon of the syrup.

3. To make the mousse: combine the chocolates, liqueur, and 3 tablespoons water in a heatproof bowl over a saucepan of very hot, but not boiling water, stirring occasionally until the chocolate is melted and the mixture is smooth.

4. Remove the bowl from the heat and allow chocolate to cool slightly. In a large bowl using a whisk, beat the egg yolks until well combined. Using a rubber spatula, blend a small amount of the warm chocolate into the yolks to temper them and prevent them from scrambling. Add the rest of the chocolate, mix with the spatula until smooth.

5. In the bowl of an electric mixer, combine the egg whites and the sugar and whip to soft peaks. Add about a quarter of the whites to the chocolate mixture and whisk them in to lighten the mixture. Then, using a rubber spatula, gently but thoroughly fold the rest of the whites (about a third at a time) into the chocolate mixture. Clean the mixer bowl, then whip the cream to soft peaks. Fold the whipped cream, (about a third at a time) into the mousse, folding until the mixture is smooth and there are no white streaks. Spoon into a glass serving bowl or individual serving dishes. Cover with plastic wrap and chill for at least 3 hours or overnight. To make the orange cream: place the cream, liqueur, and reserved syrup in a bowl and whip to soft peaks with an electric mixer. Pipe or spoon the orange cream decoratively over the mousse, then heap the candied zest over the cream.

When I am melting chocolate that I know I will be adding to egg yolks, I bring a saucepan of water to a boil, turn the heat off, and suspend a metal bowl covered with plastic wrap over the hot water. This will keep the chocolate from getting too hot and prevent you from scrambling the eggs

almond cantuccini

1. Position a rack in the center of the oven and preheat to 350 degrees. Line a baking sheet with parchment and set aside.

2. Put the flour, sugar, baking powder, cinnamon, and salt in a large bowl and stir with a rubber spatula to mix. Stir in the almonds.

3. Whisk the eggs and vanilla together in a small bowl, then stir them into the flour mixture. The dough may seem dry at this point, but it will come together as it is kneaded.

4. Turn the dough out onto a lightly floured work surface and knead, folding it over onto itself until it is smooth, 1 to 2 minutes. Divide the dough in half and shape each half into a 12-inch long log. Gently press down on the logs to flatten them until they are about 2 inches wide and 1 inch tall. Transfer them to the prepared pan.

· 2 cups all-purpose flour
· ¾ cup sugar
· 2 teaspoons baking powder
· ½ teaspoon cinnamon
· ¼ teaspoon salt
· 1 ½ cups unblanched whole almonds
· 3 large eggs

makes 4 dozen cantuccini

BAKING

First baking: Bake the logs for about 30 minutes, or until they are slightly risen and firm to the touch. Slide the logs, parchment paper and all, off the baking sheet and onto a cooling rack. The logs must be completely cool before you can continue with the recipe. Since they will take about 30 minutes to cool, you can either turn the oven off or leave it on for the next step.

Second baking: When the logs have cooled completely, preheat the oven to 350 degrees, if necessary. Line two baking sheets with parchment paper. Using a sharp serrated knife, cut the cooled logs diagonally into ¼ -inch-thick slices. Place the sliced cookies on the pans and bake for 10 to 15 minutes, or until crisp and golden. Cool on the pans. Storing: These cantuccini will keep for up to a month in an airtight container.

chocolate pudding pots with whipped cream

1. Place the chocolate in a blender. Whisk the milk, 1 cup cream, egg yolks, granulated sugar, and salt in a heavy-bottomed saucepan over medium heat. Cook, stirring constantly with a heatproof spatula until the mixture is thick enough to coat the spatula and almost boiling, 5 to 6 minutes.

2. Immediately pour the milk mixture over the chocolate in the blender. Cover and hold the lid with a thick kitchen towel; blend until combined and smooth, stopping to scrape down the sides of the blender as needed. Divide the chocolate mixture among ramekins or small cups and refrigerate until set, about 2 hours.

3. Whip the remaining ½ cup cream and the confectioners' sugar with a mixer until soft peaks form. Top the chilled pots with whipped cream. Garnish with shaved chocolate.

· 9 ounces bittersweet chocolate, chopped
· 1 ½ cups whole milk
· 1 ½ cups heavy cream, divided
· 6 large egg yolks
· 5 tablespoons granulated sugar
· ¼ teaspoon salt
· 1 tablespoon confectioners' sugar

serves 6 - 8

This simple dessert is always a hit and looks very special.

tiramisu

1. Dip ladyfingers into espresso and line them into an 8x8-inch serving dish

2. Mix cheese, sugar, vanilla, and cognac together and layer half of the cheese filling over the ladyfingers. Dust with unsweetened cocoa powder.

3. Layer with ladyfingers again and repeat cheese layer.

4. Finish by covering top layer with unsweetened cocoa. Chill 1 hour before serving.

NOTE: Tiramisu may be made the day before. Add final layer of unsweetened cocoa just before serving.

· ½ cup espresso
· 1 package ladyfingers
· 8 ounces mascarpone cheese
  (Italian cream cheese)
· ½ cup sugar
· 1 teaspoon vanilla
· 2 tablespoons cognac

serves 6

I begged for this recipe from the chef at Nino's, one of my favorite restaurants in Rome. He was very excited to share it and with a great deal of gesturing, told me all of his secrets. It's so easy and by far, the best I've ever made..

chocolate cloud cake

CAKE

1. Preheat the oven to 350 degrees. Line the bottom of an 8-inch springform pan with a round of wax paper; do not butter the pan. Melt the chocolate in a double boiler or in a bowl set over hot water. Remove from the heat and whisk in the butter until melted; set aside.

2. In a bowl, whisk the whole eggs and the 4 egg yolks with ½ cup of the sugar, just until blended. Whisk in the warm chocolate mixture. Whisk in the liqueur and the orange zest.

3. In another bowl, with an electric mixer, beat the 4 egg whites until foamy. Gradually add the remaining ½ cup sugar and beat until the whites form soft mounds that hold their shape but are not quite stiff. Stir about ¼ of the beaten egg whites into the chocolate mixture to lighten it. Gently fold in the remaining whites. Pour the batter into the pan, smooth the top.

4. Bake until the top of the cake is puffed and cracked and the center is no longer wobbly, usually 35 to 40 minutes. Do not overbake.

5. Cool the cake in the pan on a wire rack. The cake will sink as it cools, forming a crater with high sides. Don't let this part scare you.

6. Whip the cream and spread on top of the cake. Top with chocolate curls.

CAKE

- 8 ounces bittersweet chocolate, coarsely chopped
- ½ cup (1 stick) unsalted butter, cut into pieces, softened
- 6 large eggs; 2 whole, 4 separated
- 1 cup sugar, divided
- 2 tablespoons cognac or Grand Marnier
- 1 teaspoon orange zest
- 1 cup heavy cream
- Chocolate curls

serves 8-12

CHOCOLATE CURLS

Melt 4 ounces bittersweet chocolate over simmering water. Turn a jelly-roll pan over and pour the chocolate over the entire surface. Spread all the way to the edges. Refrigerate. Remove from the refrigerator and using the backside of a knife, scrape into curls.

PROFITEROLES
- 1 quart vanilla ice cream (may substitute coffee ice cream)
- ¾ stick unsalted butter, cut into pieces
- ¾ cup water
- ¼ teaspoon salt
- ¾ cup all-purpose flour
- 3 large eggs

CHOCOLATE SAUCE
- ½ cup sugar
- 1 cup heavy cream
- 7 ounces bittersweet chocolate, finely chopped
- ½ teaspoon vanilla
- 1 tablespoon brandy

serves 6

French bistros all over Paris feature this dessert. I like it because everything can be done ahead of time.

profiteroles with vanilla ice cream & chocolate sauce

PROFITEROLES

1. Chill a small metal baking pan in the freezer. Form 18 ice cream balls with ice cream scoop and freeze in chilled pan at least 1hour.

2. Preheat the oven to 425 degrees with rack in the middle. Butter a large baking sheet or line with parchment paper.

3. Bring butter, water, and salt to a boil in a small heavy saucepan, stirring until butter is melted. Reduce heat to medium, then add flour all at once and cook, beating with a wooden spoon until mixture pulls away from side of pan and forms a ball, about 30 seconds. Transfer mixture to a bowl and cool slightly, 2 to 3 minutes.

4. Add the eggs one at a time, beating well with an electric mixer after each addition. Transfer warm mixture to a pastry bag and pipe 18 mounds (about 1 ½ inches wide and 1 inch high) 1 inch apart on baking sheet.

5. Bake until puffed and golden brown, 20 to 25 minutes total. Prick each profiterole once with a tester, then return to oven to dry, propping oven door slightly ajar, 3 minutes. Set baking sheet on a rack to cool.

CHOCOLATE SAUCE

1. Heat sugar in a 2-quart heavy saucepan over medium heat, swirling pan occasionally so sugar melts evenly until it is dark amber.

2. Remove from the heat, then add cream and a pinch of salt (mixture will bubble and steam). Return to the heat and cook, stirring until caramel has dissolved. Remove from the heat and add the chocolate, whisking until melted, then whisk in vanilla and brandy. Keep warm, covered.

TO SERVE

Halve the profiteroles horizontally, and then fill each with a ball of ice cream. Put 2 or 3 profiteroles on each plate and drizzle generously with warm chocolate sauce.

CHOCOLATE BANANA BREAD

· ½ cup unsalted butter, at room temperature

· 1 cup sugar

· 2 large eggs

· 3 ripe bananas, mashed with a fork

· 1 teaspoon vanilla

· 1 ¼ cups all-purpose flour

· 1 teaspoon baking powder

· ¼ cup good quality cocoa

· ½ cup buttermilk

· 6 ounces bittersweet chocolate, chopped

BANANA CARAMEL SAUCE

· 1 cup sugar

· 2 tablespoons water

· 2 cups heavy cream

· 2 ripe bananas, peeled and sliced

BREAD PUDDING

· 4 large egg yolks

· 3 large eggs

· ½ cup sugar

· 1 pint half and half

· 1 teaspoon vanilla

serves 12

chocolate banana bread pudding with banana-caramel sauce

1. To prepare the banana bread, preheat the oven to 350 degrees. Lightly grease the bottom and sides of a 9x5-inch loaf pan. In the bowl of an electric mixer fitted with the paddle, beat together the butter and sugar until light and fluffy, about 2 minutes. Beat in eggs, adding them 1 at a time. Add bananas and vanilla.

2. Sift together the flour, soda, and cocoa onto a piece of waxed paper. Add about ⅓ of the flour mixture to the banana mixture, mix well. To the banana mixture, add ½ of the buttermilk, and then another ⅓ of the flour mixture. Repeat until all of the banana mixture, buttermilk and flour mixture are mixed well. Add chopped chocolate and mix until just combined. Turn into the prepared pan and bake until a tester comes out clean, about 1 hour. Cool and remove from the pan. Cut chocolate banana bread into 1-inch cubes and set aside.

TO PREPARE THE BREAD PUDDING
Preheat oven to 325 degrees. Butter the bottom and sides of a 9x13-inch baking pan. Evenly spread the banana bread cubes in the bottom of the pan. In the bowl of an electric mixer whisk the egg yolks, whole eggs, and sugar at medium speed until pale yellow in color, about 3 to 5 minutes. Reduce the speed to low and add the half and half and vanilla. Whisk until thoroughly combined. Pour the egg mixture over the bread cubes and press down with the back of a spatula until the bread is evenly coated. Cover the pan with aluminum foil and bake until the custard is set, about 1 hour. Cool slightly, cut into squares, and transfer to plates.

TO PREPARE THE CARAMEL SAUCE
In a medium-sized heavy saucepan, combine the sugar and water, cook over medium-high heat until the sugar dissolves. Increase the heat to high and cook, not stirring at all, until the mixture turns dark amber in color, about 10 minutes. Standing back (the mixture will splatter), carefully and gradually add the cream, and then the bananas. Continue cooking until the cream is well incorporated and the bananas are just soft. Ladle warm sauce over each serving of bread pudding and serve immediately.

apple clafouti with hot cider sauce

1. Preheat oven to 375 degrees.

2. Peel and slice the apples. Melt the butter in a sauté pan and add the apples, ¼ cup sugar, and brandy. Cook and stir gently until just cooked through. Set aside.

3. In the blender make the batter by combining ½ cup sugar, the eggs, cream, vanilla, butter, and flour. Set aside.

4. Put a 10-inch pie plate in oven to get it hot. Brush hot pie plate with butter. Pour in half of the batter. Add the apples, saving a spoonful for the top. Add the remaining batter. Top with remaining apples and any juices. Sprinkle with sugar and cinnamon.

5. Bake 25 to 30 minutes or just until set. Serve hot or cold with a little heavy cream and/or cider sauce.

HOT CIDER SAUCE
Reduce 2 quarts of good apple juice or cider by letting it boil rapidly in a wide pan until it is slightly thick or it coats a spoon. This amount will yield about 1 cup when reduced enough. It will thicken more when it cools. Spoon over each serving, on top of the cream if used.

· 6 cups Golden Delicious apples
· ¼ cup butter
· ¾ cup sugar, divided
· 3 tablespoons brandy
· 3 eggs
· 1 cup whipping cream
· 1 teaspoon vanilla
· 3 tablespoons butter, melted
· ⅔ cup flour
· 1 teaspoon cinnamon
· 1 tablespoon sugar

serves 6

Clafouti is a classic French dessert made with cherries. Try using apples, pears, or peaches.

orange polenta cake with whipped crème fraiche

1. Preheat the oven to 350 degrees. Combine 6 tablespoons sugar and 3 tablespoons water in 10-inch diameter ovenproof skillet with 8-inch-diameter bottom and 2 ½-inch-high sides. Stir over medium heat until sugar dissolves. Increase heat and boil without stirring until syrup is golden amber. Remove skillet from heat and whisk 2 tablespoons butter into caramel. Set aside.

2. Cut off both rounded ends of each orange so that ends are even and flat. Using a sharp knife, cut oranges into 1/16 to ⅛-inch-thick rounds. Remove and discard any seeds. Arrange orange slices, overlapping slightly, in concentric circles on top of the caramel in the bottom of the skillet.

3. Whisk flour, polenta, baking powder, and salt in a medium bowl to blend. Using electric mixer, beat ¾ cup sugar, remaining 6 tablespoons butter, and vanilla in another medium bowl until light and fluffy. Add egg yolks (1 at a time), beating well after each addition. Add flour mixture in 3 additions alternately with milk, beating just until batter is incorporated.

4. Using clean, dry beaters, beat egg whites in a large bowl until soft peaks form. Add remaining 1 tablespoon sugar and beat until stiff but not dry. Fold ½ of the egg whites into batter to lighten, and then fold in remaining egg whites. Drop batter by large spoonfuls on top of the orange slices in the skillet, then spread evenly.

5. Bake cake until tester inserted into center comes out clean, about 45 minutes. Cool cake in the skillet 10 minutes. Run

- · 7 tablespoons plus ¾ cup sugar, divided
- · 3 tablespoons water
- · 8 tablespoons unsalted butter, room temperature, divided
- · 2 unpeeled small to medium oranges
- · ¾ cup plus 3 tablespoons all-purpose flour
- · 3 tablespoons polenta or coarse yellow cornmeal
- · 1 ½ teaspoons baking powder
- · ¼ teaspoon salt
- · ¾ teaspoon vanilla
- · 2 large eggs, separated
- · 6 tablespoons whole milk
- · 1 cup chilled crème fraiche
- · 2 tablespoons sugar

This easy version of the pineapple upside-down cake gets a big "Wow!" using oranges.

small knife around cake to loosen. Place platter on top of the skillet. Using oven mitts, hold platter and skillet firmly together and invert, allowing cake to settle onto platter. Rearrange any orange slices that may have become dislodged. Cool cake completely at room temperature.

6. Using an electric mixer beat chilled crème fraiche and 2 tablespoons sugar in medium bowl until mixture thickens. Cut cake into wedges and serve with the whipped crème fraiche.

chocolate-pecan pie

1. Preheat the oven to 350 degrees.

2. Measure the flour, salt, and sugar into the bowl of a food processor. Add the bits of butter until they begin to resemble coarse meal. Add the ice water one tablespoon at a time until the mixture becomes a dough.

3. Press into a flat disk, wrap in plastic, and refrigerate. On a lightly floured surface, roll the dough into a 12-inch circle. Transfer to a deep 10-inch glass pie pan. Crimp the edge and refrigerate 30 minutes.

4. Toast the pecans until fragrant. Cool, then break into small pieces and transfer to a large bowl. Chop the chocolate into rough, half-inch pieces and add to the bowl, along with the flour. Stir until everything is well coated. In a food processor or mixer, cream the butter and brown sugar until light and fluffy, about 3 minutes. Add the eggs one at a time, letting each be completely incorporated before adding the next. Beat in the corn syrup, molasses, brandy, vanilla, and salt.

5. Pour the filling over the chocolate and pecans and stir well. Pour the mixture into the pie shell and bake until a tester inserted into the center is withdrawn clean, about 1 hour.

6. Cool completely on a wire rack. Serve slices of the pie at room temperature or slightly warm, topped with whipped cream.

PASTRY
- 1 ½ cups flour
- ¾ teaspoon sugar
- ¼ teaspoon salt
- 8 tablespoons unsalted butter, cut into bits
- 3 tablespoons ice water

FILLING
- 2 cups pecan halves
- 6 ounces bittersweet chocolate
- 3 tablespoons flour
- ¾ cup (6 ounces) butter, room temperature
- 1 cup dark brown sugar, firmly packed
- 5 large eggs, room temperature
- ¾ cup light corn syrup
- ¼ cup molasses
- 1 ½ tablespoons brandy
- 2 ¼ teaspoons vanilla extract
- ½ teaspoon salt

serves 10

Adding chocolate to the traditional pecan pie . . . just takes it to a whole new level!

PASTRY

- 2 cups all-purpose flour
- 1 tablespoon sugar
- ½ teaspoon salt, divided
- 1 ½ sticks cold unsalted butter, cut into small pieces
- ¼ cup ice water

APPLE FILLING & STREUSEL TOPPING

- ½ cup plus 2 tablespoons all-purpose flour
- ¼ cup walnuts, finely chopped
- ¼ cup granulated sugar
- 2 tablespoons dark brown sugar
- ½ teaspoon salt
- ⅛ teaspoon ground cinnamon
- 7 tablespoons unsalted butter, divided
- 1 cup pure maple syrup, plus more for serving
- 1 vanilla bean, split and scraped
- 5 Granny Smith apples, peeled, cored, and sliced ½-inch thick
- 1 large egg, beaten with
- 1 tablespoon of water

- Vanilla ice cream

serves 8

apple crostata with brown butter streusel & ice cream

1. In a food processor, pulse the flour, sugar, and salt. Add the butter and pulse until it is the size of small peas. Add the water and pulse just until a dough forms. Turn out onto a work surface and gather together. Shape into a disk, wrap in plastic, and refrigerate 30 minutes.

2. In a medium bowl, mix the flour with the walnuts, granulated and brown sugars, ¼ teaspoon of the salt, and the cinnamon. In a small skillet, cook 5 tablespoons of the butter over moderately high heat until golden brown, 2 minutes. Pour the butter over the walnut mixture and toss gently until crumbly. Refrigerate the streusel.

3. Preheat oven to 375 degrees. In a large skillet, bring the 1 cup of maple syrup to a simmer with the vanilla bean and seeds. Cook over moderately high heat for 3 minutes. Whisk in the remaining 2 tablespoons of butter and ¼ teaspoon of salt. Add half the apples to the skillet and cook until beginning to soften, 6 minutes. Using a slotted spoon, transfer the apples to a platter. Repeat with the remaining apples; let cool. Discard the vanilla bean and scrape the pan juices into a bowl.

4. On a lightly floured work surface, roll out the pastry to a 15-inch round, about ⅛ inch thick. Brush the egg wash in a 2-inch band around the edge of the dough. Spread the apples on the pastry; add any pan juices to the bowl. Fold the border over the apples in the center and brush the pastry with the egg wash. Sprinkle streusel on top.

5. Bake the crostata for 50 minutes, or until golden brown. Let cool slightly, then serve with ice cream drizzled with the reserved pan juices and maple syrup.

orange segments with amaretto & almond biscotti

- 6 navel oranges, segmented, white pith removed
- Amaretto liqueur
- Chocolate chunks

This is a really easy dessert that I love to do at the end of any meal. Place orange segments on a dessert plate and pour amaretto over the top. Break up chunks of a very good chocolate bar and place a few pieces on the plate.

Serve with biscotti and espresso.

winter

- 1 tablespoon soft butter or canola spray
- 1 tablespoon sugar
- 3 ½ ounces semisweet chocolate
- 2 tablespoons brewed espresso
- 3 tablespoons cornstarch
- 1 cup milk
- ⅓ cup sugar
- 3 eggs, separated, plus 2 egg whites
- 2 tablespoons soft butter
- A dash of salt
- Confectioners' sugar

CRÈME ANGLAISE
- ¼ cup granulated sugar
- ¼ teaspoon salt
- 2 large eggs
- 2 cups whole milk
- 1 teaspoon vanilla
- ⅛ teaspoon almond extract

serves 8
makes 2 cups

hot chocolate soufflé with crème anglaise

1. Spread the tablespoon of soft butter or canola spray over the bottom and sides of a 6-cup soufflé dish.

2. Sprinkle the sugar over all to coat evenly. Chill the dish. Put the chocolate and coffee together in the top of a double boiler and melt until smooth. Remove the pan from the heat and set aside.

3. Put the cornstarch into a small saucepan and pour in a small amount of the milk to dissolve the cornstarch. When well mixed, add the remaining milk and the sugar. Cook this mixture over medium heat until it thickens and comes to a boil. Remove from heat and stir in the melted chocolate mixture. Transfer this to a small bowl and set aside.

4. Separate the eggs, putting the whites in a bowl for the electric mixer. Add the two additional egg whites. The two extra egg yolks can be used in the crème anglaise.

5. Lightly beat egg yolks into the chocolate mixture, mixing thoroughly. Stir in the 2 tablespoons of butter. Preheat the oven to 375 degrees and make sure the rack is in the exact center. Add the salt to the egg whites and beat them on high speed until firm peaks form. Fold them gently into the chocolate mixture and spoon the mixture into the prepared soufflé dish. Soufflé can be completely made ahead and chilled. Make sure the rim of the dish is very clean so soufflé will go straight up.

6. Bake the soufflé in the preheated oven for 40 minutes. Serve at once with the confectioners' sugar sprinkled on the top and the sauce passed in a separate sauceboat.

CRÈME ANGLAISE

1. Combine sugar, salt, and eggs in a large bowl, stirring well with a whisk.

2. Heat the milk in a small, heavy saucepan over medium-high heat until tiny bubbles form around the edge (do not boil). Gradually add milk to egg mixture, stirring constantly with a whisk. Return milk mixture to the pan. Cook over medium-low heat for 5 minutes or until slightly thick and mixture coats the back of a spoon, stirring constantly. Remove from heat and stir in extracts. Serve chilled.

chocolate ganache tarts with toasted pecan crust

FOR THE CRUST
Preheat the oven to 325 degrees. Finely grind pecans, sugar, and cinnamon in a food processor. Add the butter and process until moist clumps form. Press dough onto bottom and sides of four 4-inch diameter tart pans with removable bottoms. Bake the crusts until golden brown and firm, about 30 minutes. Transfer to a rack and cool completely.

FOR THE FILLING
Bring cream to a simmer in a medium saucepan. Remove from the heat. Add chocolate; stir until melted and smooth. Pour the mixture into crusts. Chill until set, about 1 hour or overnight.

FOR THE TOPPING
Arrange raspberries over tops of tarts. Stir jam in a heavy small saucepan over low heat until melted. Brush melted jam over raspberries.

CRUST
· 2 cups toasted pecans
· 6 tablespoons brown sugar, lightly packed
· ¼ teaspoon ground cinnamon
· ¼ cup unsalted butter, melted

FILLING
· ¾ cup whipping cream
· 6 ounces bittersweet or semisweet chocolate, chopped

TOPPING
· 2 ½ pint baskets raspberries
· ¼ cup seedless raspberry jam

serves 4

This dessert is so easy . . . but when you serve it, your guests will go crazy!

- ⅓ cup sugar plus additional for sprinkling
- 5 ounces bittersweet chocolate, chopped
- 3 large egg yolks at room temperature
- 6 large egg whites
- Pinch of salt

serves 2

classic chocolate soufflé

1. Preheat the oven to 400 degrees. Generously butter a 2-cup soufflé dish and sprinkle with sugar, knocking out the excess.

2. Melt chocolate in a metal bowl set over a saucepan of barely simmering water, stirring occasionally until smooth. Remove bowl from heat and stir in yolks (mixture will stiffen).

3. Beat whites with a pinch of salt in a large bowl with an electric mixer at medium speed until they just hold soft peaks. Add ⅓ cup sugar, a little at a time, continuing to beat at medium speed, and then beat at high speed until whites just hold stiff peaks. Stir about 1 cup whites into chocolate mixture to lighten, and then add mixture to remaining whites, folding gently but thoroughly.

4. Spoon into soufflé dish and run the end of your thumb around inside edge of soufflé dish (this will help soufflé to rise evenly). Bake in middle of oven until puffed and crusted on top but still jiggly in the center, 20 minutes. Serve immediately.

NOTE: A soufflé, quickly described, is a sauce containing a flavoring or puree into which stiffly beaten egg whites are incorporated. It is turned into a mold and baked in the oven until it puffs up and the top browns. The glory and lightness of soufflé are largely a matter of how voluminously stiff the egg whites have been beaten and how lightly they have been folded into the body of the soufflé. It is the air, beaten into the whites, which expands as the soufflé is cooked and pushes it up into its magnificent puff. The egg whites should be 7 to 8 times their original volume. The very famous French Chef Escoffier always finished his soufflé lessons with a wave of the arm proclaiming that the "soufflé waits for no one; you must wait for the soufflé."

pears poached in red wine with crème fraiche

1. Fill a large bowl with cold water and add the teaspoon of lemon juice. Peel the pears with a vegetable peeler, cut them in half lengthwise, and carefully scoop out the core and stem. As they are peeled and cored, drop them into the acidulated water to prevent them from darkening.

2. When all the pears have been prepared, put the lemon and orange juices, rind strips, wine, sugar, cinnamon sticks, cloves, and fresh cold water into a deep kettle. Bring this mixture to a rapid boil. Reduce the heat to simmer and gently drop the pears into the wine syrup. Cover the pot, reduce to very low, and poach the pears in the barely simmering liquid about 10 minutes or until they seem tender when stabbed with a toothpick. Do not overcook them; they should have some resistance.

3. Cool the pears in the pot and then refrigerate them. The longer the pears chill in the wine syrup, the better. Put the wine syrup in a saucepan and reduce to very thick syrup.

4. Put a pear half into a small dessert bowl. Spoon some of the thickened wine syrup over the pear. Place a dollop of the crème fraiche on top and sprinkle with crushed amaretti cookies.

CREME FRAICHE
Whip the heavy cream with the sugar, vanilla, and cinnamon until it is thick and stiff. Gently fold in the sour cream.

· 1 teaspoon lemon juice
· 4 fresh pears
· Rind of 1 lemon and 1 orange, removed in long strips
· Juice from the lemon and orange
· 1 bottle red wine
· 2 cups sugar
· 4 sticks cinnamon
· 6 whole cloves
· 6 cups cold water

CREME FRAICHE
· 1 cup heavy cream
· 2 teaspoons sugar
· 1 teaspoon vanilla
· 1 teaspoon ground cinnamon
· 1 cup sour cream
· Crushed amaretti cookies

serves 8

January is the perfect month for pears. Remember to choose firm, but ripe, pears and start the recipe the day before serving. Marinating overnight in the wine mixture is just as important as the poaching and gives the pears their beautiful claret color. The pears can be marinated for several days.

bourbon pumpkin pie with pecan streusel & whipped cream

1. Preheat the oven to 350 degrees. In a medium bowl, combine 4 tablespoons of the butter and ¼ cup of the brown sugar with the flour and pinch into moist crumbs. Stir in the pecans.

2. In a large bowl, using an electric mixer, beat the remaining stick of butter and ¾ cup brown sugar at medium speed until light and fluffy, about 1 minute. Beat in the pumpkin puree, egg yolks, cornstarch, cinnamon, nutmeg, cloves, and salt. Then beat in the milk and bourbon.

3. In a stainless steel bowl, using clean beaters, beat the egg whites until stiff but not dry, then fold into the pumpkin mixture until no white steaks remain.

4. Pour the custard into the pasty shell. Sprinkle the pecan streusel on top. Bake the pie in the middle of the oven for 1 hour, or until risen and golden and a tester inserted into the center comes out with only a few moist crumbs attached. Let cool and serve.

5. Serve with whipped cream or ice cream.

· 1 ½ sticks unsalted butter at room temperature, divided
· 1 cup dark brown sugar, packed, divided
· ½ cup all-purpose flour
· ½ cup pecan halves
· 1 ¼ cup canned pumpkin puree
· 3 large eggs, separated
· 1 ½ tablespoons cornstarch
· ½ teaspoon cinnamon
· ¼ teaspoon freshly grated nutmeg
· ¼ teaspoon ground cloves
· ¼ teaspoon salt
· ½ cup milk
· ¼ cup bourbon

· 1 basic recipe for pastry
· 1 cup whipping cream

makes one 10-inch tart or pie

cranberry-tequila cream cheese tart with cornmeal crust

FOR THE CRUST

1. Mix the flour, cornmeal, sugar, and salt in the bowl of a food processor. Add the butter and pulse until mixture resembles coarse meal. Add the cream cheese and pulse to combine. Add enough ice water until a dough forms. Gather into a ball. Roll out the dough to fit 11 or 12-inch tart pan with removable bottom. Fold in excess dough to form double-thick sides. Transfer the tart pan to the freezer and chill for 30 minutes.

2. Preheat the oven to 350 degrees. Line with foil and pie weights. Bake for about 15 minutes. Remove the foil and bake for 20 more minutes. Transfer to a rack and let crust cool completely in pan.

FOR THE FILLING

Using the electric mixer beat cream cheese and butter in a large bowl until light. Beat in the powdered sugar, then the remaining ingredients. Spread cream cheese filling evenly in the crust. Refrigerate until filling sets, about 2 hours.

FOR THE GLAZE

1. Combine the sugar, orange juice concentrate, butter, liqueur, cinnamon, and allspice in a medium saucepan over high heat. Boil 2 minutes. Add the cranberries. Return to a boil. Boil for 1 minute. Transfer the glaze to a bowl and cool completely.

2. Spoon glaze over filling. Cover and refrigerate until firm, about 4 hours. (Can be prepared 1 day ahead. Keep refrigerated.) Garnish tart with orange peel.

CRUST
- 1 cup flour
- ⅔ cup yellow cornmeal
- 1 teaspoon sugar
- Pinch of salt
- 1 stick chilled unsalted butter, cut into pieces
- ⅔ cup cream cheese, chilled, cut into pieces
- 3 tablespoons ice water

FILLING
- 8 ounces cream cheese, room temperature
- 1 stick butter, room temperature
- 1 cup powdered sugar
- 1 tablespoon plus
- 2 teaspoons Cointreau or other orange liqueur
- 1 tablespoon plus
- 1 teaspoon tequila
- 1 tablespoon grated orange peel
- ¼ teaspoon salt

CRANBERRY GLAZE

- ¾ cup sugar
- ⅓ cup frozen orange juice concentrate
- 2 tablespoons butter
- 2 tablespoons Cointreau or other orange liqueur
- ½ teaspoon ground cinnamon
- ¼ teaspoon ground allspice
- 2 cups fresh cranberries

- Orange peel strips

serves 12

I love this dessert for Christmas!

chocolate espresso almond torte

1. Preheat the oven to 350 degrees. Place a large pan filled halfway with water on the stove over medium heat. Place the chocolate and butter in a metal bowl and set it in the pan with the water. Gently whisk together until melted. Remove from heat and set aside.

2. Beat together the eggs and sugar on high speed, until mixture is pale yellow. Gently stir in the melted chocolate mixture, cocoa, instant coffee, and almond extract.

3. Pour the batter into a 9-inch springform pan that has been lightly sprayed with cooking spray. Bake for 10 minutes. Cover with foil and bake another 15 minutes. Remove from oven and set aside to cool.

4. To make the espresso cream, beat together the whipping cream, sugar, and coffee until extremely thick. Spoon over cooled torte, cover with plastic wrap, and refrigerate overnight.

5. To serve, cut into pieces and top with cocoa powder sprinkled through a strainer. Then add chopped almonds.

TORTE
- 16 ounces bittersweet chocolate, finely chopped
- 2 sticks unsalted butter, cut into pieces
- 5 large eggs
- ½ cup sugar
- ¼ cup dark chocolate cocoa
- ¼ cup instant coffee granules
- 1 teaspoon almond extract

ESPRESSO CREAM
- 2 cups heavy whipping cream
- 1 cup powdered sugar
- 3 tablespoons freshly made strong coffee, cooled

TOPPING
- ¼ cup cocoa powder
- Toasted almonds, chopped

serves 10

Easy . . . beautiful . . . delicious

crepes suzette

1. Blend the flour, egg, yolks, salt, and milk for a few seconds. Add the melted butter, 1 tablespoon sugar, and vanilla and blend well. Refrigerate for 30 minutes.

2. Heat the frozen butter in a 7 or 8-inch skillet. Pour a small amount of the batter into the skillet and immediately swirl it around to completely coat the bottom. Let it cook for a minute or two and then flip. Place the crepes between parchment papers to keep them from sticking. You should get 24 crepes.

3. To make the Suzette butter, put the ¼ cup sugar, orange and lemon zest and juice, Grand Marnier, and butter into a small saucepan and heat until the butter is bubbly.

4. Have a shallow gratin dish ready for the crepes. Brush each crepe with the melted butter mixture, fold it in half, brush again, and fold it into a fan shape, and then brush the entire outside of the folded crepe. Place it in the dish and continue brushing and folding the crepes. Arrange them slightly overlapping in the dish and pour any extra butter mixture over the top. At this point the dish can be refrigerated for several days until you are ready to bake it.

5. To bake, bring the crepes to room temperature. Preheat the oven to 400 degrees. Sprinkle powdered sugar over the top of the crepes and bake them for 15 to 20 minutes or until the tops are crisp and bubbly. Bring the hot dish to the table and pour about ¼ cup of warmed Grand Marnier over the crepes. Ignite and while the flame dies, serve the crepes with the juices spooned over.

· 1 cup flour
· 1 whole egg
· 2 egg yolks
· Dash of salt
· 1 ½ cups milk
· 3 tablespoons melted butter
· 1 tablespoon sugar
· 1 teaspoon vanilla extract
· 8 tablespoons butter, frozen
· ¼ cup sugar
· Zest and juice of 1 large orange
· Zest and juice of 1 lemon
· ¼ cup Grand Marnier
· 8 tablespoons butter

serves 8

Impress your friends and serve this dessert on New Year's Eve. Make it the day before, then wow them by lighting it before serving.

chocolate brownies with peanut butter cream

1. Preheat the oven to 350 degrees. Line a 13x9x2-inch baking pan with aluminum foil, leaving 2-inch overhang on both short sides. Spray foil with non-stick spray. Combine both chocolates and butter in small saucepan. Stir over low heat until melted and smooth. Cool to barely lukewarm. Using an electric mixer, beat sugar, eggs, and vanilla extract in a large bowl on high speed until mixture thickens and is pale yellow, about 5 minutes. Reduce mixer speed to low; beat in flour and salt, then melted chocolate mixture. Fold in walnuts. Transfer mixture to prepared baking pan.

2. Bake the brownies until tester inserted into center comes out with moist crumbs still attached, about 20 minutes. Transfer baking pan to a rack; cool 15 minutes. Press gently on edges of brownies to level with center. Cool completely in baking pan.

3. Combine the peanut butter and butter in medium bowl. Using electric mixer, beat until smooth. Add powdered sugar and vanilla extract and beat until well blended and smooth. Spread butter cream evenly over brownies in pan. Refrigerate at least 1 hour. Using foil as aid, lift out brownies from pan. Cut into squares. Optional serving: spoon a dollop of peanut butter cream on top of each brownie.

BROWNIES
· Non-stick vegetable spray
· 5 ounces unsweetened chocolate, coarsely chopped
· 4 ounces bittersweet chocolate, coarsely chopped
· ½ cup (1 stick) unsalted butter
· 1 ½ cups sugar
· 4 large eggs
· 1 teaspoon vanilla extract
· ½ cup all-purpose flour
· ¼ teaspoon salt
· ½ cup chopped walnuts

PEANUT BUTTER CREAM
· 1 cup creamy peanut butter
· 3 tablespoons unsalted butter, room temperature
· ⅔ cup powdered sugar
· 1 teaspoon vanilla extract

makes 24

bananas foster

1. Melt the butter in a flat chafing dish or skillet. Add the brown sugar and stir until sugar is melted. Add bananas and sauté until tender, about 3 minutes on each side. Sprinkle with cinnamon. Pour rum over bananas, shake pan to distribute the liquid, and flame. Baste bananas with the flaming sauce until flame dies out.

2. Serve immediately over the ice cream or yogurt.

· 8 tablespoons unsalted butter
· 8 tablespoons brown sugar
· 6 ripe bananas, peeled and sliced lengthwise
· ½ teaspoon cinnamon
· 4 tablespoons dark rum
· Ice cream, frozen yogurt, or crème fraiche

serves 6

Bananas Foster is a winner in any season. It's easy and always delicious.

bittersweet chocolate cake soufflés

1. Preheat oven to 350 degrees. In a large mixing bowl, cream butter and sugar until fluffy. Add eggs, one at a time, mixing well after each addition. Add melted chocolate and espresso, mix well.

2. In a small bowl, mix flour, baking soda, and salt. Add half of the sour cream to the chocolate mixture, mix well. Add half the flour mixture and mix again. Repeat. Add vanilla and mix.

3. Grease six 3 ½-ounce ramekins and fit with foil collars. Distribute the batter among the ramekins. Bake for 25 minutes, or until a tester inserted in the center comes out clean. Serve warm.

4. For the chocolate ganache, bring ½ cup heavy cream to a boil and pour over 6 ounces chopped bittersweet chocolate. Stir until melted. Drizzle over the soufflés and garnish with whipped cream and chocolate shavings.

SOUFFLES
- ½ cup unsalted butter, softened
- 2 ¼ cups brown sugar
- 3 eggs
- 12 ounces bittersweet chocolate, melted
- 1 cup hot espresso
- 2 cups flour
- 2 teaspoons baking soda
- Pinch salt
- 1 cup sour cream

CHOCOLATE TOPPING
- ½ cup heavy cream
- 6 ounces bittersweet chocolate, chopped

GARNISH
- Whipped cream
- Chocolate shavings

serves 8

PASTRY
- 1 ½ cups all-purpose flour
- ½ teaspoon salt
- 10 tablespoons unsalted butter, cut into small cubes and chilled
- 4 to 5 tablespoons ice water

FILLING
- 5 to 6 Granny Smith apples, peeled, cored, and quartered
- 1 teaspoon cinnamon
- 1 cup sugar, divided
- 4 tablespoons unsalted butter, cut into small pieces

SWEETENED CRÉME FRAICHE
- 1 cup crème fraiche
- 2 to 4 tablespoons heavy cream
- 2 to 4 tablespoons sugar
- 1 teaspoon vanilla extract

makes one 10-inch tarte

I love this delicious upside down apple pie. It is a classic French bistro staple.

apple tarte tatin with sweetened crème fraiche

FOR THE PASTRY

1. Place the dry ingredients into the bowl of a food processor and pulse until mixed. Add the butter one piece at a time until the mixture resembles coarse meal. Add the ice water until the mixture becomes a dough, forms into a ball, and pulls away from the sides of the work bowl. Wrap in plastic wrap and put in the refrigerator until ready to use.

2. On a lightly floured surface, roll the dough into a 12-inch circle. Trim rough edges, if necessary, to maintain a round shape. Transfer to a sheet pan, cover with plastic wrap, and refrigerate.

3. Preheat the oven to 400 degrees.

FOR THE FILLING

1. Toss the apples with the cinnamon and ¼ cup of the sugar.

2. In a 10-inch cast-iron pan or other heavy based, ovenproof skillet, heat the remaining ¾ cup sugar over medium-high heat, until the sugar turns dark amber. Add the butter and stir it into the caramel until melted.

3. Remove the pan from the heat. Beginning on the outside of the pan, carefully set the apple quarters in the caramel, arranging them in a circle so that they all face the same way. Set them very close to one another. Fill in the center of the pan with as many of the remaining apples as will fit. Put the pan back on the heat and allow the apples to cook on the stove for about 5 minutes. Remove the pan from the heat. Place the cold pie dough over the apples, tucking the edges into the sides of the pan. Work carefully so as not to burn your fingers, but also quickly so as not to melt the dough. Brush the dough with the beaten egg and immediately put in the oven.

4. Bake for 15 minutes. Lower the temperature to 375 degrees and bake until the crust is nicely browned and the caramel is bubbling around the edges of the pan, another 15 minutes. Carefully remove the tart from the oven and cool it on a rack for about 20 minutes. Invert the tart onto a serving platter. If any apples stick to the underside of the pan, simply return them to their rightful spot on the tart. Tarte Tatin is best served right away with sweetened crème fraiche.

texas chocolate cream pie

1. Preheat oven to 350 degrees. Place the chocolate wafers into the bowl of a food processor. Add the melted butter and sugar. Process until smooth. Press onto the bottom and the sides of a 10-inch tart pan or 9-inch pie plate. Bake until crisp, about 15 minutes; cool on a wire rack.

2. Whisk together sugar, cornstarch, salt, and yolks in a 3-quart saucepan until combined well, then add milk in a steady stream, whisking the whole time. Bring to a boil over moderate heat, whisking, then reduce heat and simmer, whisking for 1 minute. The filling will be very thick.

3. Put the filling through a fine-mesh sieve into a bowl, then whisk in chocolates, butter, and vanilla. Cover surface of the filling with plastic wrap and cool completely for 2 hours.

4. Spoon the filling into a crust and chill for at least 6 hours.

5. Just before serving, beat cream with the sugar in the bowl of an electric mixer just until it holds stiff peaks, then spoon on top of the pie. Garnish with shaved chocolate.

CRUST
- 1 ⅓ cups chocolate wafer crumbs
- 5 tablespoons unsalted butter, melted
- ¼ cup sugar

FILLING
- ⅔ cup sugar
- ¼ cup cornstarch
- ½ teaspoon salt
- 4 large egg yolks
- 3 cups whole milk
- 5 ounces bittersweet chocolate, melted
- 2 ounces unsweetened chocolate, melted
- 2 tablespoons unsalted butter, softened
- 1 teaspoon vanilla

TOPPING
- 1 cup heavy cream
- 1 tablespoon sugar

serves 8

blackberry pie with sour cream whipped cream

1. Put the 2 ½ cups flour into the bowl of a food processor with ½ teaspoon salt. Add the butter one tablespoon at a time until the mixture resembles a coarse meal. Add about 10 tablespoons ice water until the mixture forms into a ball and pulls away from the bowl of the food processor. Halve the dough into 2 disks. Wrap separately in plastic wrap and refrigerate for about 1 hour.

2. Unwrap 1 dough disk; transfer to a lightly floured work surface and roll out to form an 11-inch circle. Transfer to a 9-inch deep dish pie pan or a 10-inch tart pan. Chill.

3. Preheat the oven to 425 degrees. Put berries, ¾ cup sugar, lemon juice, zest, remaining flour, and salt into a bowl. Using a wooden spoon, mash gently to make a textured filling; pour into chilled crust, dot with 1 tablespoon butter, and set aside.

4. Beat egg white and 1 tablespoon water together in a bowl and set aside. Roll out remaining dough disk into an 11-inch circle, cut into ¾-inch wide strips. Arrange strips over pie in a lattice pattern; trim excess dough and crimp edges of pie. Brush crust with egg mixture and sprinkle with remaining sugar. Bake on the middle rack of the oven until crust is just golden, about 15 minutes. Reduce heat to 350 and bake until golden brown and bubbling, about 30 minutes more.

5. Beat the whipping cream to stiff peaks and fold in the sour cream. Serve with the pie at room temperature.

· 2 ½ cups plus ⅓ cup flour
· 2 sticks unsalted butter
· 1 teaspoon salt, divided
· 6 cups blackberries
· ¾ cup plus 2 tablespoons sugar
· 2 teaspoons fresh lemon juice
· ½ teaspoon lemon zest
· 1 egg white

· 1 cup heavy cream
· ¼ cup sour cream

serves 8

PRALINE
- 1 cup whole blanched almonds
- ¾ cup sugar
- ¼ cup water

CAKE
- 3 ounces bittersweet chocolate
- ⅓ cup unsweetened cocoa powder
- 5 tablespoons unsalted butter
- ⅓ cup vegetable oil
- ⅔ cup water
- 1 cup plus
- 2 tablespoons sugar
- 1 large egg
- 1 ¼ cups all-purpose flour
- 2 teaspoons baking powder
- ⅓ cup well-shaken buttermilk
- 8 ounces mascarpone cheese, at room temperature
- 1 ½ tablespoons sugar

serves 8

chocolate cake with mascarpone & praline

FOR THE PRALINE

Preheat the oven to 350 degrees. In a baking pan, toast nuts in one layer in middle of oven 10 minutes, or until almonds are lightly colored. Wrap in a kitchen towel and let steam 1 minute. Line a baking sheet with foil. In a small heavy saucepan bring sugar and water to a boil, stirring until sugar is dissolved. Boil syrup, without stirring, until it begins to turn golden. Swirl pan until syrup is deep golden and remove from heat. Stir in nuts and pour praline onto baking sheet, spreading evenly. Cool praline completely and break into pieces. Transfer praline to a sealable plastic bag and coarsely crush with a rolling pin.

FOR THE CAKE

1. Preheat the oven to 300 degrees. Generously butter a 9-inch round cake pan and line bottom with parchment paper. Butter paper and dust pan with flour, knocking out excess. Finely chop chocolate. In a small saucepan combine cocoa powder, butter, oil, and water. Bring to a boil, stirring until smooth, and remove pan from heat. Add chocolate and sugar, whisking until smooth, and transfer to a bowl. Cool chocolate mixture completely and whisk in egg. Sift flour and baking powder over chocolate and whisk until just combined. Whisk in buttermilk and pour batter into cake pan, spreading evenly.

2. Bake cake in middle of oven 45 to 50 minutes, or until a tester comes out clean and cool in pan on a rack 5 minutes. Run a thin knife around edge of pan and invert cake onto a rack. Discard paper. Cool cake completely and transfer to a plate.

3. In a bowl stir together mascarpone and sugar. Spread mixture over top of cake, or spoon a dollop onto each serving, and sprinkle generously with praline pieces.

french bread pudding with whiskey sauce

1. Preheat oven to 350 degrees.

2. In a large bowl, cream together the sugar and butter. Add eggs, cream, cinnamon, vanilla, and raisins, mixing well. Pour into a 9-inch square pan 1 ¾ inches deep.

3. Arrange bread slices flat in the egg mixture and let stand for 5 minutes to soak up some of the liquid. Turn bread over and let stand for 10 minutes longer. Then push bread down so that the egg mixture covers most of it.

4. Set pan in a larger pan filled with water to ½ inch from top. Cover with aluminum foil. Bake for 45-50 minutes, uncovering pudding for the last 10 minutes to brown the top. When done, the custard should still be soft, not firm.

5. To make the sauce: In a saucepan combine sugar, 1 cup cream, cinnamon, and butter. Bring to a boil. Add in the cornstarch mixed with the ¼ cup water and cook, stirring, until sauce is clear. Remove from heat and stir in whiskey.

6. To serve, spoon the warm pudding onto dessert plates and pass the sauce separately.

· 1 cup sugar
· 8 tablespoons (1 stick) butter, softened
· 5 eggs, beaten
· 1 pint (2 cups) heavy cream
· Dash of cinnamon
· 1 tablespoon vanilla extract
· ½ cup raisins
· 12 slices, each 1-inch thick, of French bread, fresh or stale

WHISKEY SAUCE
· 1 cup sugar
· 1 cup heavy cream
· 1 cinnamon stick or a dash of ground cinnamon
· 1 tablespoon unsalted butter
· ½ teaspoon cornstarch
· ¼ cup additional water
· 1 tablespoon bourbon

serves 6 - 8

banana pudding with toasted meringue

1. Heat milk in top of a double boiler set over simmering water. In a small bowl, whisk together ¾ cup sugar, cornstarch, egg yolks, and enough water to make a soup paste (about ¼ cup). Whisk egg yolk mixture into milk. Cook, stirring constantly until thickened to the consistency of pudding, 15 - 20 minutes. Remove from the heat, stir in butter and vanilla. Let cool slightly.

2. Preheat the oven to 325 degrees. Cover bottom of a 9x13-inch baking dish with half the vanilla wafers. Slice the bananas into ½-inch-thick rounds and spread half of them over wafers. Cover bananas with half the pudding. Spread remaining wafers over pudding, followed by remaining bananas. Pour rest of the pudding over the top.

3. Place egg whites and cream of tartar in a chilled metal bowl. Using an electric mixer on slow to medium speed, beat until soft peaks form. Add the remaining sugar (1 tablespoon at a time) and continue to beat until stiff, but not dry, peaks form to make a meringue. Spread meringue over pudding and bake until lightly browned, 20 to 30 minutes. Serve warm, at room temperature, or chilled.

· 4 cups milk
· ¾ cup plus
· 3 tablespoons sugar
· ¼ cup cornstarch
· 4 eggs, separated, plus 2 egg whites
· 4 teaspoons unsalted butter
· 2 teaspoons vanilla extract
· 1 12-ounce box vanilla wafers
· 3 - 4 firm bananas
· ¼ teaspoon cream of tartar

Banana pudding always reminds me of home, with a couple of differences. My mom used Jell-O pudding and did not top it with meringue. Sure does dress up this comfort dessert, huh?

spring

LIME MOUSSE
· 1 ½ teaspoons unflavored gelatin
· 1 ½ tablespoons cold water
· ½ cup fresh lime juice
· 2 ½ teaspoons finely grated
  fresh lime zest
· ¼ cup plus ⅓ cup sugar
· 1 large egg white
· 1 cup well-chilled heavy cream
· 2 pints strawberries

TART SHELL
· ¼ cup whole blanched almonds
· 1 large egg
· 1 vanilla bean
· 5 tablespoons unsalted butter,
  softened
· ¼ cup confectioners' sugar
· ⅛ teaspoon salt
· 1 cup flour

serves 8

FOR THE MOUSSE

1. In a small bowl sprinkle gelatin over 1 ½ table-spoons cold water and let soften 1 minute. In a small saucepan heat gelatin mixture, lime juice, zest, and ¼ cup sugar over moderately low heat, stirring, just until sugar and gelatin are dissolved, then cool to room temperature.

2. Set a metal bowl over a saucepan and put enough water in pan so that bottom of bowl just touches the water. Remove bowl from pan and bring water to a boil. In a bowl stir together egg white and remaining ⅓ cup sugar with a spoon until combined. Remove pan of boiling water from heat and immediately set bowl over pan. Stir egg mixture gently with spoon 1 minute (keep mixture as froth-free as possible because the froth cooks more quickly).

3. With an electric mixer, beat egg mixture at high speed 5 minutes, or until cool. Reduce speed to medium and beat meringue 3 minutes more, or until it holds tiny peaks. In another bowl beat cream until it holds soft peaks. Gradually stir lime mixture into meringue until combined. (Mixture will be thin and not completely smooth.) Fold in whipped cream gently but thoroughly.

4. Spoon mousse into tart shell, smoothing top. Chill tart, uncovered, at least 4 hours, or until mousse is set and covered, up to 1 day.

5. Trim strawberries and arrange, cut sides down, over tart. Gently gather threads of spun sugar together and arrange over tart. (See recipe for spun sugar.)

FOR THE TART SHELL

1. In a spice grinder finely grind almonds. In a small bowl lightly beat egg. Split vanilla bean lengthwise, and scrape seeds into a bowl. Add butter, confectioners' sugar, and salt, and beat un-til smooth with an electric mixer. Beat in ground almonds and 3 tablespoons beaten egg, beating until smooth; stir in flour until just combined. Discard remaining egg. Gather dough into a ball and flatten into a disk. Chill dough. Roll out dough to a 12-inch round. Place in a 9-inch tart pan with removable bottom. Chill shell for about 20 minutes.

2. Preheat the oven to 375 degrees. Line the shell with foil and pie weights, place pan on baking sheet and bake until deep golden, about 15 minutes. Cool shell on baking sheet on a rack. May make 1 day ahead and keep wrapped in plastic wrap at room temperature.

1. Cover a work surface with parchment paper. In a small saucepan bring sugar and water to a boil over moderate heat. Boil syrup, without stirring, until very pale golden. Remove pan from heat, swirling caramel gently until it stops cooking. Cool caramel, without stirring, until thick enough to drizzle in a thin thread, about 8 minutes.

2. In one hand hold 2 forks back to back and dip tines into caramel, letting excess caramel drip back into pan. Rapidly wave forks back and forth over parchment to form threads. Repeat procedure with remaining caramel. Spun sugar may be made a day ahead and kept in an airtight container at room temperature.

· Parchment paper
· 1 cup sugar
· ¼ cup water

Spinning the sugar is so much fun. It turns a really easy dessert into something spectacular!

CAKE
- 6 eggs, separated
- ¾ cup sugar
- 6 tablespoons cocoa
- 2 teaspoons vanilla extract
- 1 teaspoon almond extract
- 1 teaspoon ground cinnamon
- 1 teaspoon ground star anise, anise extract, or licorice flavored aperitif

FILLING
- 2 cups heavy cream
- ½ cup sugar
- 4 tablespoons cocoa
- 1 teaspoon vanilla extract

GARNISH
- Chopped pistachio nuts or shaved chocolate for garnish

serves 8

I couldn't do a dessert book without including this recipe. It was the first dessert I learned when taking cooking class from Cheri Zitron in New York. It was her favorite and became mine as well. It can be done two days ahead and still looks beautiful.

1. Preheat the oven to 350 degrees. Line an 11x16-inch jellyroll pan with butter, parchment paper, and more butter. Trim the paper leaving an overhang on each side. Set pan aside.

2. Beat the egg yolks thoroughly, and gradually add the sugar. Continue beating until the mixture is very thick and creamy. Add the cocoa, vanilla, almond extract, cinnamon, and anise. Beat thoroughly. Beat the egg whites in a separate bowl until they hold firm peaks. Fold them into the cocoa mixture. Pour the batter into the prepared pan and bake for 25 minutes or until the sides of the cake pull away from the pan.

3. Turn the cake over immediately onto a damp linen kitchen towel, remove the parchment paper and roll the cake up in the towel. Set aside to cool thoroughly, at room temperature.

4. While the cake is cooling, put all of the ingredients for the filling into a bowl and set the bowl and beaters into the refrigerator to chill thoroughly.

5. When ready to fill and serve the cake, beat the cream mixture thoroughly until whipped.

6. Unroll the cake and spread about ½ of the mixture over the cake. Roll up the cake.

7. Spread the remaining filling over the top to frost the cake completely. If desired, save about ½ cup of the cream for a pastry bag to decorate the cake with rosettes of cream. Sprinkle with pistachio nuts or shaved chocolate and serve.

Preheat the oven to 450 degrees.

FOR THE PASTRY

Place the flour and salt in the bowl of a food processor. Add the cold butter and shortening until the mixture resembles a fine meal consistency. Slowly add the water until the mixture forms into a ball and pulls away from the sides of the bowl. Remove, divide in half, and wrap in plastic wrap. Place in the refrigerator for about 30 minutes while preparing the filling.

FOR THE FILLING

1. Whisk together granulated sugar, cornstarch, tapioca, and salt. Toss with the berries. Roll out one piece of the pastry on a lightly floured work surface and place into a 9-inch pie pan. Trim the edge and leave a ½-inch overhang. Roll out remaining piece of pastry to an 11-inch round.

2. Spoon the filling into pie shell, cover with the second pastry round, and trim. Press edges together and crimp. Brush top of the pie with beaten egg and sprinkle with raw sugar. Cut 3 steam vents in the top of the crust.

3. Bake for 15 minutes, then reduce temperature to 375 degrees and continue to bake for 45 minutes. Cool for at least 3 hours to allow the juices to thicken. Serve with lemon-mascarpone cream. To make the cream, place the mascarpone cheese, cream, sugar, and lemon zest and juice in the bowl of an electric mixer. Whip on medium speed until soft peaks form. Keep chilled until ready to use.

PASTRY
· 2 ½ cups all-purpose flour
· 1 ½ sticks cold unsalted butter, cut into cubes
· ¼ cup cold vegetable shortening
· ½ teaspoon salt
· 4 to 6 tablespoons water

FILLING
· 1 cup granulated sugar
· 3 tablespoons cornstarch
· 2 tablespoons quick cooking tapioca
· ¼ teaspoon salt
· 3 cups blackberries
· 2 cups raspberries
· 2 cups blueberries
· 1 egg, lightly beaten
· 1 tablespoon raw sugar, Demerara, or Turbinado sugar

LEMON-MASCARPONE CREAM
· 4 ounces mascarpone cheese
· 1 cup heavy cream
· 2 tablespoons sugar
· Zest and juice of one lemon

serves 8

jam crostata

1. In the bowl of a food processor, mix together the all-purpose flour, cake flour, sugar, lemon zest, and salt. Slowly drop the butter through the feed tube piece by piece. Gradually add the beaten egg until a soft dough forms. Gather the dough into a ball and flatten into a disk. Wrap in plastic and refrigerate until firm.

2. Preheat the oven to 350 degrees. Using a knife cut two-thirds of the dough from the disk; wrap the rest in plastic. Roll out the dough to a 10-inch round and place into a 9-inch tart pan with a removable bottom. Refrigerate the shell. Roll out the remaining dough into a 9x6-inch rectangle. Refrigerate until chilled. Spoon the jam into the tart shell and spread it evenly. Cut the dough rectangle lengthwise into 12 strips. Arrange half of the strips across the tart; for a decorative look, twist the strips first. Working in the opposite direction, repeat with the remaining strips to form a lattice. Brush the lattice with the egg yolk wash.

3. Bake the tart on the bottom rack of the oven for 30 minutes, or until the crust is golden brown and crisp. Serve at room temperature.

· 1 cup all-purpose four
· ½ cup cake flour
· ¼ cup sugar
· ½ teaspoon lemon zest, finely grated
· Pinch of salt
· 8 tablespoons unsalted butter, cut into pieces
· 1 large egg, beaten
· 1 ½ cups jam or preserves (14 ounces)
· 1 large egg yolk, beaten with 1 or more teaspoons water

makes one 9-inch tart

Make this tart with any favorite jam. Dust with powdered sugar before serving.

lemon bars

1. Preheat the oven to 350 degrees.

2. In a food processor cream together the butter, flour, confectioners' sugar, and salt until they form a ball. With your fingers, press the dough into the bottom of a lightly buttered 8-inch baking pan. Bake for 20 minutes.

3. Prepare the lemon topping while shortbread is baking.

4. Beat eggs well, gradually adding the sugar. While continuing to beat the eggs and sugar, slowly add the remaining ingredients.

5. Reduce oven to 325 degrees. Pour topping over the hot, baked shortbread and return to the oven at once.

6. Bake for 30-35 minutes, until the top is light gold.

7. Remove the pan, run a sharp knife around the edges and cool for about 20 minutes. Cut into squares, remove from pan, and sprinkle with confectioners' sugar.

SHORTBREAD
· ½ cup butter (1 stick), at room temperature
· 1 cup all-purpose flour
· ¼ cup confectioners' sugar
· Pinch of salt

LEMON TOPPING
· 2 eggs
· 1 cup sugar
· ¼ teaspoon salt
· Juice and zest of 2 lemons
· 1 ¼ cup flour

serves 8

red velvet cupcakes with coconut & cream cheese frosting

1. Preheat oven to 350 degrees. Line 18 muffin cups with paper liners. Sift flour and cocoa into small bowl. Using an electric mixer, beat 1 ½ cups sugar and ¾ cup butter in a large bowl until smooth. Beat in eggs one at a time, then ⅔ cup buttermilk, red food coloring and 1 teaspoon vanilla. Mix in dry ingredients in 3 additions. Make well in center; pour in remaining ⅓ cup buttermilk, vinegar, and baking soda. When bubbles form stir in batter.

2. Divide batter equally among paper liners. Bake cupcakes until tester inserted into center comes out clean, about 20 minutes. Cool 10 minutes; transfer to a rack and cool completely.

3. Beat cream cheese, ¼ cup butter, and remaining 1 teaspoon vanilla in a medium bowl until smooth. Beat in powdered sugar; fold in 1 cup flaked coconut. Spread frosting on cupcakes, leaving ½-inch plain border; sprinkle with remaining 1 cup coconut.

- 1 ¾ cups flour
- ¼ cup unsweetened cocoa powder
- 1 ½ cups sugar
- 2 sticks unsalted butter, room temperature, divided
- 2 large eggs
- 1 tablespoon red food coloring
- 2 teaspoons vanilla extract, divided
- 1 cup buttermilk, divided
- 1 teaspoon distilled white vinegar
- ¼ teaspoon baking soda
- 2 8-ounce packages cream cheese, room temperature
- 1 ½ cups powdered sugar
- 2 cups sweetened flaked coconut, divided

makes 18

french apple turnovers with crème fraiche

1. Preheat the oven to 400 degrees.

2. Peel, core, and cut the apples into 1-inch pieces. Place the apples in a medium saucepan; add the water, sugar, and lemon juice. Bring to a boil, stirring occasionally until sugar dissolves. Cook the apples until they are very tender, about 10 minutes. Remove from the heat and gently mash with a fork until the mixture is soft, but still chunky. Cool completely.

3. Place some of the filling into the center of each pastry square. Lightly brush edges of 1 pastry with the beaten egg. Fold half of pastry square over filling, forming a triangle. Press and pinch pastry edges with fingertips to seal tightly. Lightly brush pastry with beaten egg. Sprinkle with the sugar. Repeat with remaining squares and filling. Place on a baking sheet covered with parchment paper. Refrigerate until firm, about 15 minutes.

4. Bake the turnovers for 15 to 20 minutes until golden and puffed. Serve with crème fraiche

FILLING
- 1 pound Granny Smith apples
- 1 pound Golden Delicious apples
- ½ cup water
- 4 tablespoons sugar
- 2 teaspoons fresh lemon juice

- Puff pastry squares
- 1 egg
- Sugar
- 1 cup crème fraiche

makes 10 turnovers

Puff pastry can be filled with jams, preserves, or one of my favorites, a chunk of chocolate and orange zest. Try it!

1. For the crust: Preheat the oven to 350 degrees and butter bottom and side of 9-inch springform pan. Stir together crumbs, sugar, and butter in a bowl with a fork until combined well, then press evenly onto bottom and one-third up side of pan. Bake crust in the middle of oven 10 minutes and cool in pan on a rack.

2. Reduce oven temperature to 325 degrees.

3. Beat cream cheese in the bowl of a food processor; add the sugar. Add lime juice, sour cream, and vanilla. Mix until smooth. Mix in flour and salt at low speed, scraping down side as needed, until just incorporated, then add eggs all at once and mix just until incorporated.

4. Pour filling into crust and set springform pan in a shallow baking pan. Bake cake in middle of oven until set in center, 1 hour to 1 hour and 10 minutes. Cool completely in springform pan on rack. Run a thin knife around edge of cake and remove side of pan.

5. Peel mangoes and, leaving fruit whole, slice very thinly lengthwise with a vegetable peeler. Halve wide slices lengthwise. Gently toss mango slices with lime juice.

6. Beat cream with sugar in a bowl with electric mixer until it just holds stiff peaks, then spread over top of cheesecake. Bending and curling mango slices, arrange them decoratively over cream. Garnish with lime zest.

CRUST
- 1 ¼ cups fine graham cracker crumbs
- 3 tablespoons sugar
- ½ stick unsalted butter, melted

FILLING
- 2 (8-ounce) packages cream cheese at room temperature
- 1 cup plus 2 tablespoons sugar
- ¾ cup fresh lime juice
- ½ cup sour cream
- ½ teaspoon vanilla
- 2 ½ tablespoons all-purpose flour
- ½ teaspoon salt
- 3 large eggs

TOPPING
- 2 large firm, ripe mangoes
- 1 tablespoon fresh lime juice
- ½ cup chilled heavy cream
- 1 tablespoon sugar
- Grated lime zest for garnish

NOTE: To avoid craters in your cheesecake, wrap the springform pan with foil. Place in a pan with about one inch of water, then bake. This really works.

crème fraiche panna cotta with berries

1. Place the milk in a large bowl, sprinkle the gelatin over it, and stir to combine.

2. In a medium saucepan, bring the cream and 5 tablespoons sugar to a boil. Lightly oil eight 4-ounce ramekins or a large gratin dish.

3. When the cream mixture comes to a boil, turn off the heat and let it sit for a few minutes. Slowly whisk the cream into the gelatin, and then whisk in the crème fraiche. Strain the mixture and pour it into the prepared ramekins. Chill in the refrigerator for at least 3 hours or longer.

4. A few minutes before serving, place the berries in a bowl and toss with a tablespoon of sugar. Run a knife around the edges of the panna cotta and invert it onto a large chilled platter. Surround with the berries and their juice.

· ½ cup cold whole milk
· 3 ½ teaspoons unflavored gelatin (¼ -ounce package)
· 3 cups heavy cream
· 6 tablespoons granulated sugar, divided
· Canola spray for ramekins
· ½ cup plus
· 2 tablespoons crème fraiche
· 1 ½ pints fresh raspberries, strawberries, blackberries, or blueberries

serves 8

Panna cotta is a favorite Italian dessert. Easy, do-ahead, light and the perfect ending.

lemon mousse with blackberries

1. Melt butter in a double boiler, or in a stainless steel bowl set over a saucepan of simmering water. (Do not let the bottom of the bowl touch the water.) In a separate bowl, whisk eggs, sugar, and lemon juice until smooth. Add egg mixture to the melted butter. Heat slowly, whisking constantly, until mixture thickens to the consistency of pudding. Strain through a fine sieve into a separate bowl. Cool completely in the refrigerator.

2. In another bowl, whip heavy cream and lemon zest to stiff peaks. Fold into cooled egg mixture. Spoon into wineglasses or dessert bowls and chill. Garnish with a dollop of whipped cream and blueberries.

· 4 tablespoons unsalted butter
· 3 large eggs
· ½ cup sugar
· ⅓ cup fresh lemon juice
· 1 cup heavy cream
· Zest of 2 lemons, finely chopped
· ¼ cup heavy cream, whipped
· 1 pint blueberries, blackberries, or raspberries

serves 6

1. Put ¾ cup of the sugar and ¼ cup water in a pot and set over high heat. Cook, swirling the pan occasionally, until the color turns medium amber. Carefully pour the caramel into a 9-inch round nonstick cake pan.

2. Arrange the pineapple slices in a single layer over the caramel.

3. Preheat the oven to 350 degrees.

4. In a large bowl, beat the butter and remaining 1 cup of the sugar until light and fluffy. In another bowl, whisk together the eggs and yolks. Beat the egg mixture into the butter. Combine the flour, cornmeal, baking powder, and salt in a sieve and sift them over the bowl. Stir until the batter is smooth and well blended. Spread the batter over the fruit in the pan.

5. Bake 40 to 45 minutes, or until a tester inserted in the center of the cake comes out clean. Invert the cake onto a plate.

6. In a medium saucepan, combine all of the sauce ingredients. Bring to a simmer and stir well.

7. In a medium saucepan, heat the rum over medium heat. Carefully pour the rum over the cake. It may ignite.

8. Serve the cake while still warm, drizzled with the warm sauce.

NOTE: You can also bake the cake in individual molds. It goes well with ice cream or pineapple sorbet. Make the sauce ahead and store it in the refrigerator, well wrapped. It keeps well for a long time.

CAKE
- 1 ¾ cups sugar, divided
- 6 slices fresh pineapple (½-inch thick), cored
- 12 tablespoons unsalted butter, at room temperature
- 3 eggs
- 6 egg yolks
- ¾ cup all-purpose flour
- ⅔ cup cornmeal
- ¾ teaspoon baking powder
- Pinch of salt

SAUCE
- 1 ½ cups unsweetened coconut milk
- 1 cup unsweetened pineapple juice
- ¾ cup canned sweetened cream of coconut, such as Coco Lopez

GARNISH
- ½ cup white rum

This is a classic—adding the sauce gives a tropical flavor.

key lime cupcakes

1. Preheat the oven to 350 degrees. Line a standard muffin pan with 12 paper liners. Whisk both flours in a medium bowl. Beat butter in a large bowl until smooth. Add sugar; beat to blend. Beat in the eggs 1 at a time, then the lime juice, zest, and food coloring. Batter may look curdled.

2. Beat in flour mixture in 3 additions alternately with buttermilk in 2 additions. Spoon ⅓ cup batter into each liner.

3. Bake cupcakes until tester inserted into center comes out clean, 20 to 25 minutes. Cool 10 minutes. Remove from pan; cool.

4. Beat all of the ingredients for the frosting in a medium bowl until smooth. Spread over cupcakes.

CUPCAKES
· 1 cup all-purpose flour
· ¾ cup self-rising flour
· 1 stick unsalted butter, room temperature
· 1 ¼ cups sugar
· 2 large eggs
· 2 ½ tablespoons fresh key lime or regular lime juice
· 1 tablespoon lime zest, finely grated
· ¼ teaspoon neon-green food coloring
· ¾ cup buttermilk

FROSTING
· 1 8-ounce package cream cheese, room temperature
· 1 ½ cups powdered sugar
· 1 stick unsalted butter, room temperature
· 1 tablespoon lime zest, finely grated
· ½ teaspoon vanilla extract

makes 12

Beautiful for Easter!

1. In the bowl of an electric mixer, beat cream cheese until smooth. Add sour cream, confectioners' sugar, lime zest, lime juice, tequila, and triple sec; beat until combined. In another bowl, whip heavy cream until stiff peaks form; fold into cream cheese mixture. Cover with plastic wrap; freeze until firm, about 30 minutes.

2. Pulse granulated sugar and graham crackers in a food processor until finely chopped; stir in melted butter. To serve, place lime juice on one plate and salt on another. Dip rims of glasses in juice, then graham cracker crumbs. Remove mixture from freezer and scoop into glasses; sprinkle with graham cracker topping. Let soften slightly before serving.

- 12 ounces cream cheese, room temperature
- ½ cup sour cream
- ⅔ cup sifted confectioners' sugar
- 2 tablespoons finely grated lime zest
- 4 tablespoons freshly squeezed lime juice, plus more for glasses
- 4 tablespoons tequila
- 4 tablespoons triple sec
- 1 cup heavy cream
- 4 tablespoons granulated sugar
- 8 graham crackers
- 4 tablespoons unsalted butter, melted

serves 8

blueberry-lemon shortcakes with lemon cream

1. Simmer 3 cups blueberries, sugar, water, and lemon juice in a saucepan over medium heat. Cook, stirring occasionally, until berries burst and sauce has thickened, about 10 minutes. Off the heat, stir in remaining blueberries.

2. To assemble, spoon some berry sauce in the center of each plate. Sandwich a scoop of ice cream between each halved biscuit, set biscuits in the sauce on each dish and drizzle with more berry sauce. Top with lemon cream and strips of lemon zest.

LEMON CREAM
Beat cream to stiff peaks in a large bowl with a hand mixer. Add sour cream, blend to combine, and then stir in sugar and zest. Chill up to 2 hours before serving.

- 6 cups fresh blueberries, divided
- 1 cup sugar
- ½ cup water
- 2 tablespoons fresh lemon juice
- Vanilla ice cream
- 1 can buttermilk biscuits, cooked according to package, then split
- Strips of lemon zest

LEMON CREAM
- 1 cup heavy cream
- 1 cup sour cream
- 4 tablespoons powdered sugar
- 2 teaspoons minced lemon zest

makes 8 shortcakes

lemon-honey semifreddo

1. Line a 9x4 ½ x 3-inch loaf pan with plastic wrap, allowing at least 3 inches of overhang on the long sides. In a small bowl, sprinkle the gelatin over the water and let stand.

2. In a medium bowl, using an electric mixer, beat the egg whites at high speed until firm peaks form. In another bowl, beat the cream until firmly whipped; refrigerate.

3. In a large bowl set over a pot of simmering water, beat the egg yolks with the honey at medium speed until thickened and about 160 degrees, about 5-6 minutes. Remove the bowl from the pot and beat in the gelatin mixture, lemon juice and zest; continue beating until slightly cooled, about 5 minutes longer.

4. Using a spatula, fold in the beaten egg whites and whipped cream into the lemon-honey mixture until no streaks remain. Pour half of the semifreddo base into the prepared loaf pan. Arrange the ladyfinger sandwiches in the pan in 2 long rows and top with the remaining semifreddo base. Cover loosely with the overhanging plastic wrap and freeze until firm, at least 4 hours or overnight. Unmold the semifreddo and peel off the plastic wrap; slice and serve.

· 1 teaspoon gelatin
· 1 tablespoon water
· 3 large egg whites
· 1 cup chilled heavy cream
· 6 large egg yolks
· ½ cup honey
· 3 tablespoons lemon juice, plus 1 teaspoon finely grated lemon zest (Meyer lemons if available)
· 12 soft ladyfingers sandwiched with orange marmalade

serves 8

PASTRY
- 3 cups all-purpose flour
- 2 teaspoons sugar
- 1 teaspoon salt
- 1 stick cold unsalted butter, cut into cubes
- ½ cup vegetable shortening
- ½ cup ice water

FILLING
- 1 stick unsalted butter, softened
- 1 ½ cups sugar
- 3 large eggs, separated
- 2 cups buttermilk
- 1 tablespoon lemon juice
- ¼ teaspoon freshly grated nutmeg
- ¼ cup all-purpose flour

HONEY CRÈME FRAICHE
- 16 ounces crème fraiche
- 2 tablespoons honey

TO MAKE THE PASTRY

1. Combine the flour, 2 teaspoons sugar, and the salt in a food processor and pulse until well combined. Add butter and shortening and continue to process until the mixture resembles coarse breadcrumbs. Add cold water and process until the dough comes together in a ball. Turn out onto a lightly floured surface and gently knead a few times until the dough is smooth. Wrap in plastic wrap and refrigerate for 20 minutes.

2. Preheat the oven to 350 degrees.

3. On a lightly floured surface, roll the dough into a 12-inch circle. Carefully roll circle of dough around your rolling pin, then unroll it on top of a 10-inch tart pan, gently pressing it around the insides of the pan. Trim any overhang and discard. Cover with a piece of foil and fill with pie weights. Bake in the middle of the oven about 20 minutes or until the crust is set and just firm. Remove weights and cool pie shell.

4. Reduce the temperature of the oven to 325 degrees.

TO MAKE THE FILLING

1. Using a mixer, beat the butter and the 1 ½ cups sugar on medium speed until light, fluffy, and pale in color. Add egg yolks, buttermilk, lemon juice, and nutmeg. Continue to mix until batter is smooth, occasionally scraping down the sides of the bowl with a rubber spatula. Add flour and continue to mix until just combined. Transfer buttermilk mixture to a separate bowl. Thoroughly wash mixing bowl and attachment with soap and hot water; using the mixer, beat egg whites on high until stiff peaks form. Gently fold egg whites, half at a time, into buttermilk mixture. Pour filling into cooled pie shell. Bake for 35 to 40 minutes, until the pie is set. Cool, and serve with honey crème fraiche.

2. Using a mixer beat the crème fraiche on high for 45 seconds, until it tightens up slightly. Fold in the honey with a spoon so it is just mixed, but you can still see swirls of honey.

espresso panna cotta with shaved white & dark chocolate

1. Place the milk in a saucepan. Sprinkle the gelatin over and let stand for 5 minutes to soften the gelatin. Stir over medium heat just until the gelatin dissolves, but the milk does not boil, about 2 minutes. Add the cream, espresso powder, sugar, and salt. Stir over low heat until the sugar dissolves, about 3 more minutes.

2. Remove from the heat and let cool slightly. Pour the cream mixture into 6 martini glasses, dividing equally. Cover and refrigerate. Chill until set, at least 6 hours and up to 2 days. When ready to serve, use a vegetable peeler on the chocolate blocks to create about 1 tablespoon each of the white and dark chocolate shavings. Sprinkle the shavings over each panna cotta and serve.

- 1 ½ cups whole milk
- 4 ½ teaspoons unflavored powdered gelatin or 2 gelatin sheets
- 4 ½ cups heavy cream
- 6 teaspoons instant espresso powder
- ¾ cup sugar
- Pinch of salt
- 1 small white chocolate bar, for garnish
- 1 small dark chocolate bar, for garnish

If you put the bars of chocolate in the microwave for 10 seconds, it will be easier to get nice shavings.

coconut crème brûlée

1. Preheat the oven to 325 degrees.

2. In a saucepan heat cream, milk, and vanilla bean over moderately high heat until mixture just comes to a boil, and then remove from heat. Steep vanilla bean 10 minutes, and with a knife, scrape seeds into milk mixture, reserving pod.

3. In a bowl, whisk together yolks, whole egg, and granulated sugar until combined well, and then add milk mixture in a stream, whisking. Skim off any froth.

4. Divide coconut and custard among eight ½-cup ramekins set in a roasting pan. Add enough hot water to pan to reach halfway up sides of ramekins.

5. Bake custards in middle of oven until they are just set but still tremble slightly, about 40 minutes. Remove ramekins from pan and cool custards. Chill, covered loosely with plastic wrap, at least 4 hours or overnight.

6. Set broiler rack so that custards will be 2-3 inches from heat and preheat broiler.

7. Sift sugar evenly over custards and broil custards until sugar is melted and caramelized, about 2 minutes. Chill custards 20 minutes.

· 1 ¾ cups heavy cream
· 1 ¾ cups milk
· 1 vanilla bean, split lengthwise
· 1 large egg
· 6 large egg yolks
· ½ cup granulated sugar
· ⅔ cup packed, flaked sweetened coconut, toasted golden, cooled, and crumbled coarse
· ¼ cup Demerara sugar (raw sugar)

serves 8

If you have a kitchen torch, this works really well. I like to serve fresh berries with this dessert.

cookies

almond-blueberry cookies

1. Preheat the oven to 375 degrees.

2. In a medium bowl, combine flour, baking powder, and salt.

3. In another medium bowl, cream together the butter and sugar using a hand mixer. Add the egg and beat to incorporate. Add the milk, almond extract, and lemon zest.

4. Stir the dry ingredients into the wet ingredients. Fold in the almonds, then the blueberries. Chill the dough in the refrigerator 30 minutes.

5. Using two small spoons, dollop dough onto cookie sheets. Bake until golden brown around the edges, about 15 minutes.

6. Cool the cookies on a wire rack. Dust with confectioners' sugar.

· 2 cups all-purpose flour
· 2 teaspoons baking powder
· ½ teaspoon salt
· 1 stick unsalted butter, room temperature
· 1 cup sugar
· 1 egg
· ¼ to ⅓ cup whole milk
· 1 teaspoon almond extract
· 2 teaspoons lemon zest, about 1 lemon
· ½ cup chopped almonds, toasted
· 1 cup frozen blueberries, thawed and drained

makes about 20 cookies

peanut butter chocolate chip cookies

1. Preheat the oven to 350 degrees. Line two baking sheets with parchment paper.

2. Cream the butter, peanut butter, and brown sugar together in a large bowl with an electric mixer until fluffy. Add the egg and vanilla and mix until all the ingredients are combined.

3. In a separate large bowl, stir the flour, baking soda, and salt together. Stir the flour mixture into the peanut butter mixture until the flour is no longer visible. Stir in the chocolate chips until evenly distributed.

4. Scoop the dough with a ¼ -cup measure or ice cream scoop and drop it onto the prepared cookie sheet leaving 3 inches between the cookies. Use a fork to flatten the tops of the cookies to ½- to ¼ -inch thickness with a crosshatch pattern.

5. Bake the cookies on a center rack for 15 to 17 minutes, rotating the pans halfway through for even baking, until the cookies are golden brown. Let the cookies cool on the baking sheet for 5 to 10 minutes before transferring them to a wire rack to cool completely.

- 8 tablespoons unsalted butter, softened
- ¾ cup creamy peanut butter
- 1 cup packed light brown sugar
- 1 large egg
- 1 teaspoon vanilla extract
- 1 ½ cups all-purpose flour
- 1 teaspoon baking soda
- ¼ teaspoon salt
- 1 cup semisweet chocolate chips

makes 2 dozen cookies

chocolate chunk oatmeal coconut cookies

1. Preheat oven to 375 degrees.

2. Beat together butter and sugars in a bowl with an electric mixer at high speed until fluffy. Add eggs and beat until just blended, then beat in vanilla, baking soda, and salt. Add flour and mix at low speed until just blended. Stir in oats, coconut, chocolate, and almonds.

3. Arrange ¼ -cup mounds of cookie dough about 3 inches apart on 2 lightly buttered large baking sheets (about 8 cookies per sheet), then gently pat down each mound to about ½ inch thick. Bake in upper and lower thirds of oven, switching position and rotating pans halfway through baking, until golden, 15 to 18 minutes total.

4. Cool cookies on sheets 1 minute, then transfer with a spatula to racks to cool completely. Make more cookies in same manner.

NOTE: You can substitute packaged chocolate chunks instead of cutting up chocolate yourself.

· 2 sticks (1 cup) unsalted butter, softened
· 1 cup packed brown sugar
· 6 tablespoons granulated sugar
· 2 large eggs
· 1 ½ teaspoons vanilla
· ½ teaspoon baking soda
· ½ teaspoon salt
· 1 cup all-purpose flour
· 2 ¼ cups old-fashioned oats
· 1 ½ cups packaged unsweetened coconut, finely shredded
· 12 ounces bittersweet chocolate, cut into ½-inch chunks
· ¾ cup almonds with skins, toasted, cooled, and chopped

makes 24 cookies

cranberry-white chocolate chunk cookies

1. Preheat the oven to 350 degrees.

2. In a mixer, combine the sugar, shortening, eggs, and vanilla. Add the flour, oats, and baking powder and mix until well combined. Gently stir in the white chocolate, cranberries, coconut, and cashews by hand. Make balls with a ¼ cup ice cream scoop and place about 2 inches apart on a baking sheet lined with a nonstick baking mat or on a lightly greased baking sheet. Pat down the balls to make ¾-inch disks.

- ½ cup granulated sugar
- ½ cup vegetable shortening
- 2 large eggs
- 1 teaspoon vanilla extract
- 1 cup all-purpose flour
- 1 cup oats
- 1 teaspoon baking powder
- 1 cup white chocolate chunks
- ½ cup dried cranberries
- ½ cup shredded coconut
- ½ cup cashew halves

makes 24 cookies

hazelnut linzer cookies with blackberry jam

1. Whisk the flour, cinnamon, baking powder, nutmeg, and salt in a medium bowl until blended.

2. Beat butter, 1 cup powdered sugar, and citrus peels in a large bowl until fluffy. Beat in egg yolks. Beat in dry ingredients in 4 additions; beat in the nuts. Gather dough into a ball; flatten into a disk. Wrap, chill at least 1 hour and up to 1 day.

3. Preheat the oven to 325 degrees. Line 2 large rimmed baking sheets with parchment paper. Roll out half of dough on lightly floured surface to ⅛-inch thickness. Using 2-inch round cutter, cut out rounds. Using ¾-inch round cutter, cut out center of half of rounds to make rings. Transfer rounds and rings to prepared sheets. Gather dough scraps; chill.

4. Bake cookies until golden, reversing sheets after 10 minutes, about 20 minutes total. Cool completely on sheets. Repeat until all dough is used.

5. Arrange cookie rings on work surface. Sift powdered sugar over. Spread 1 teaspoon jam on each cookie round. Press rings onto jam on rounds.

- 1 ¼ cups all-purpose flour
- 2 teaspoons ground cinnamon
- 1 teaspoon baking powder
- ½ teaspoon freshly grated nutmeg
- ½ teaspoon salt
- 1 ½ sticks unsalted butter, room temperature
- 1 cup powdered sugar plus more for decorating
- 5 teaspoons packed orange peel, finely grated
- 2 teaspoons grated lemon peel
- 3 large egg yolks
- 1 ¼ cups hazelnuts, finely ground in processor
- Blackberry jam

makes about 30 sandwiches

macadamia butter cookies with dried cherries

1. Preheat oven to 375 degrees.

2. Place nuts in a food processor; process until smooth, scraping sides of bowl once. Combine macadamia butter, ½ cup sugar, and brown sugar in a large bowl, beat with a mixer at medium speed. Add vanilla and egg and beat well.

3. Lightly spoon flour into dry measuring cups, level with a knife. Combine flour, baking soda, salt, and ground nutmeg, stirring with a whisk. Add flour mixture to sugar mixture; beat at low speed just until combined (mixture will be very thick). Stir in chopped cherries. Chill 10 minutes.

4. Divide chilled dough into 24 equal portions; roll each portion into a ball. Place 1 tablespoon granulated sugar in a small bowl. Lightly press each ball into sugar; place each ball, sugar side up, on a baking sheet covered with parchment paper.

5. Gently press the top of each cookie with a fork. Dip the fork in water; gently press the top of each cookie again to form crisscross pattern. Place 12 cookies on each of 2 baking sheets.

6. Bake cookies, 1 baking sheet at a time, for 10 minutes or until golden. Remove cookies from pan, cool on a wire rack. Repeat procedure with remaining cookies.

- ⅔ cup macadamia nuts
- ½ cup plus
- 1 tablespoon granulated sugar
- ½ cup packed light brown sugar
- 1 teaspoon vanilla extract
- 1 large egg
- 1 ¼ cups all-purpose flour
- ½ teaspoon baking soda
- ¼ teaspoon salt
- ⅛ teaspoon ground nutmeg
- ½ cup dried cherries, chopped

maple walnut oatmeal cookies

1. Preheat oven to 300 degrees. Line two baking sheets with parchment paper, and set aside. In a medium bowl, combine the oatmeal, coconut, flour, salt, and sugar. Set aside.

2. In a small saucepan over medium heat, combine the butter and maple syrup. Heat until the butter is melted. Remove from the heat and set aside. In a small bowl, combine the baking soda with 2 tablespoons boiling water. Immediately stir this mixture into the melted butter until combined. Add the maple extract, stir into the oat mixture. Fold in the walnuts.

3. Form dough into 2-ounce balls, about 3 tablespoons each, and place the balls onto prepared cookie sheets about 3 inches apart, six to a sheet. Flatten each of the balls slightly.

4. Bake the cookies until golden brown and set, about 20 minutes. Transfer to a wire rack to cool. Store in an airtight container up to 1 week.

· 1 ½ cups old-fashioned oatmeal
· ¾ cup flaked coconut
· 1 ⅓ cups all-purpose flour
· ½ teaspoon salt
· ⅔ cup packed light brown sugar
· ½ cup (1 stick) plus
· 1 tablespoon butter
· 5 tablespoons pure maple syrup
· 1 teaspoon baking soda
· 1 teaspoon maple extract
· 1 cup walnuts, coarsely chopped

makes 12 cookies

oatmeal cookies with dried apricots and white chocolate

1. Preheat the oven to 350 degrees.

2. Mix flour, oatmeal, and baking soda in a medium bowl. Cream butter and sugars with a mixer until light and fluffy. Reduce speed to low. Add salt, vanilla, and eggs and beat until well combined. Add flour mixture gradually, beating until just combined. Stir in chocolate and apricots. Cover and refrigerate until cold, about 30 minutes.

3. Using ¼ cup measure ice cream scoop, place dough onto parchment-lined baking sheets, spacing 2 inches apart. Bake until cookies are golden brown around the edges but still soft in the center, 15 minutes. Let cookies cool on baking sheets for 2 minutes. Transfer cookies to a wire rack; let cool. Cookies will keep, covered, for up to 1 week.

· 1 ½ cups all-purpose flour
· 1 ½ cups old-fashioned oatmeal
· ½ teaspoon baking soda
· 2 sticks unsalted butter, softened
· ¼ cup granulated sugar
· 1 cup packed light-brown sugar
· 1 teaspoon salt
· 1 teaspoon vanilla extract
· 2 large eggs
· 8 ounces white chocolate, chopped
· 1 ½ cups dried apricots, chopped

makes about 4 dozen

chocolate chip macaroons

1. Preheat the oven to 350 degrees.

2. Lightly butter 2 large baking sheets. Toast the pecans until fragrant. Transfer to a plate to cool, then chop them.

3. In a large bowl, combine the coconut with the chocolate chips, flour, salt, and pecans. Add the condensed milk and vanilla, and stir until evenly moistened.

4. Mound level tablespoons of the batter on the prepared baking sheets and bake for about 20 minutes, or until lightly golden but still moist inside. Let cool to room temperature before serving.

5. Can be stored at room temperature in an airtight container for up to 3 days.

- 1 ¼ cups pecan halves
- Two 7-ounce bags sweetened shredded coconut
- 1 ¼ cups semisweet mini chocolate chips
- ⅓ cup plus
- 1 tablespoon all-purpose flour
- ⅛ teaspoon salt
- One 14-ounce can sweetened condensed milk
- 2 ½ teaspoons pure vanilla extract

makes about 4 dozen macaroons

I love these macaroons. This recipe makes a lot, but trust me, the platter will be empty.

glossary

Almonds: The kernel of the almond tree. Almonds are grown extensively in California, the Mediterranean, Australia, and Africa.

Almond Extract: A flavoring produced by combining bitter-almond oil with ethyl alcohol. The flavor is very intense.

Almond Paste: A mixture of blanched ground almonds, sugar, and glycerin or other liquid.

Amaretti: A crisp, airy macaroon cookie.

Anise: A member of the parsley family. It has a distinct sweet licorice flavor.

Baking Powder: A leavening agent containing a combination of baking soda, an acid and a moisture absorber. When mixed with liquid, baking powder releases carbon dioxide that causes a bread or cake to rise.

Baking Soda: Also known as bicarbonate, soda is an alkali used as a leavening agent in baked goods. When combined with an acid ingredient such as buttermilk, yogurt, or molasses, baking soda produces carbon dioxide gas bubbles causing a dough or batter to rise.

Biscotti: A twice baked Italian biscuit that's made by first baking it in a loaf, then slicing the loaf and baking the slices. The result is an intensely crunchy cookie.

Brandy: A liquor distilled from wine or other fermented fruit juice. The name "brandy" comes from the Dutch brandying referring to the technique of heating the wine during distillation.

Buttermilk: It is made commercially by adding special bacteria to nonfat or low-fat milk, giving it a slightly thickened texture and tangy flavor.

Chocolate: Unsweetened- Also called baking or bitter chocolate. U.S. standards require that unsweetened chocolate contain between 50 and 58 percent cocoa butter.

Bittersweet- Must contain at least 35 percent chocolate liquor.

Semisweet- Semisweet and sweet can contain from 15 to 35 percent chocolate liquor.

Milk- Dry milk is added to sweetened chocolate and creates a milk chocolate which must contain at least 12 percent milk solids and 10 percent chocolate liquor.

White- Not true chocolate because it contains no chocolate liquor and likewise very little chocolate flavor. It's usually a mixture of sugar, cocoa butter, milk solids, lecithin, and vanilla.

Clafouti: A country French dessert made by topping a layer of fresh fruit with batter.

Corn Starch: A dense powdery "flour" obtained from the endosperm portion of the corn kernel. Cornstarch is most commonly used as a thickening agent for puddings, sauces, soups, etc.

Corn Syrup: A thick, sweet syrup created by processing cornstarch with acids and enzymes. *Light corn syrup* has been clarified to remove all color and cloudiness. *Dark corn syrup* is caramel flavor with coloring added, deeper stronger flavor.

Coulis: A general term referring to a thick puree or sauce.

Crème Anglaise: The French term for a rich custard sauce.

Crème Fraiche: Thickened cream that has a slightly tangy, nutty flavor and velvety rich texture.

Espresso: A dark, strong coffee made by forcing steam through finely ground, Italian-roast coffee especially blended for making espresso.

Evaporated Milk: Canned, unsweetened milk is fresh, homogenized milk from which 60 per cent of the water has been removed. Vitamin D is added for extra nutritional value.

Flan: A famous Spanish baked custard coated with caramel.

Flour: *All purpose-* made from a blend of high-gluten hard wheat and low-gluten soft wheat. *Bleached-* A fine-textured flour milled from the inner part of the wheat kernel and contains neither the germ nor the bran.

Cake flour (pastry flour): A fine-textured, soft wheat flour with a high starch content. Makes particularly tender cakes and pastry.

Ganache: A rich filling/icing made of chocolate and cream, heated and stirred together until the chocolate has melted.

Gelatin: An odorless, tasteless, and colorless thickening agent, which forms a jelly when dissolved in hot water and then cooled.

Gratin: Any dish that is topped with cheese or breadcrumbs, then heated in the oven or under the broiler until brown and crispy.

Kirsch: This clear brandy is distilled from cherry juice and pits.

Maple syrup: Maple tree sap that has been boiled until much of the water has evaporated to produce a thick syrup.

Mascarpone: From Italy's Lombardy region, mascarpone is a buttery-rich double cream to triple cream made from cow's milk.

Meyer Lemons: A cross between a lemon and an orange. The aromatic juice is sweeter and less acidic.

Molasses: *Light molasses* comes from the first boiling and is lighter in both flavor and color. *Dark molasses* comes from a second boiling and is darker, thicker, and less sweet.

Mousse: A French term meaning "froth" or "foam," mousse is a rich airy dish that can be either sweet or savory, hot or cold.

Panna Cotta: Italian for "cooked cream," Panna Cotta is a light, silky eggless custard.

Port: A sweet fortified wine.

Praline: A brittle confection made of almonds and caramelized sugar.

Profiterole: A miniature cream puff filled with either a sweet or savory mixture.

Roulade: A soufflé-type mixture that's spread on a jellyroll pan, baked until firm, but still moist, then spread with a savory or sweet filling and rolled up jellyroll fashion.

Shortbread: A tender, crisp butter-rich cookie.

Sugar: *Granulated-* highly refined cane or beet sugar. Most common for table use or for cooking. *Confectioners'* or *powdered sugar-* granulated sugar that has been crushed into a fine powder. *Brown sugar-* white sugar combined with molasses. *Demerara* or *turbinato-sugar-* raw sugar that has been steam-cleaned.

Soufflé: A light airy mixture that usually begins with a thick egg yolk-based sauce that is lightened by stiffly beaten egg whites. Soufflés may be savory or sweet, hot or cold.

Tapioca: A starchy substance extracted from the root of the cassava plant. It is used as a thickening agent.

Vanilla: Vanilla beans come from Madagascar. It is rich and sweet. Vanilla extract is made by macerating chopped beans in an alcohol-water solution to extract the flavor.

Vegetable Oil: May be any of various edible oils made from a plant source, such as vegetables, nuts, or seeds.

Vegetable Shortening: A solid fat made from vegetable oils. Although made from oil, shortening has been chemically transformed into a solid state.

Zuccoto: A dome-shaped dessert that begins with a bowl lined with liqueur-moistened cake slices. The bowl is then filled with sweetened whipped cream, chopped or grated chocolate, and then topped with additional cake slices.

index